Converting Political Power to Economic Power:

Our Historical Challenge

JAMES E. COVINGTON

Copyright © 2015 by James E. Covington

All rights reserved.
No part of this book may be reproduced
or transmitted in any form or by any means
without permission by the author.

ISBN-13: 978-1511770682
ISBN-10: 1511770686

Table of Contents

PART I: A Call to Action..5

PART II: Understanding Our Historical Challenge..................35
    Our Nineteenth-Century Historical Challenge:
    Slavery and the Abolition Movement...................................39
    Our Twentieth-Century Historical Challenge:
    The Civil Rights Movement..59
    Our Twenty-First-Century Historical Challenge:
    Converting Political Power to Economic Power..................84
    The Urgency of Now..119

PART III: Overcoming Our Historical Challenge...................121
    The Foundation for Solutions:
    Building the Black Business Class......................................123
    Strategies in Action:
    The Partnership for Economic Development.....................142
    Strategies in Action:
    More About WhereToGo411.com..166
    The Future Starts Now..168

    Acknowledgments...174
    About James Covington...177

PART I:

A Call to Action

This book is your call to action!

It is your call to action to understand the Historical Challenge we face as African-Americans, to understand what we must do to overcome the challenge, and to overcome it—by growing a black business class that can empower us to convert our political power to economic power.

Today, there are more African-Americans graduating from college, more receiving PhDs, more lawyers, more black professionals, and more doctors than at any point in our history in America. We sit as CEOs of major corporations, we are mayors of major cities, we have more black elected officials controlling the spending of public funds, we run colleges and universities, we lead megachurches, we head nonprofit organizations, and we own or control other economic engines. Our annual buying power continues to rise, today reaching one trillion, one hundred billion dollars—exceeding the Gross National Product of many nations.

Very few races of people, if any, can lay claim to this kind of political power—yet all across America, African-American communities are on the verge of collapse under the awesome weight of crime, joblessness, failing schools, lost hope, and too many other challenges to mention here. While these are all legitimate problems, they do not rise to the level of a Historical Challenge. In order to solve these problems, it is necessary to overcome the Historical Challenge: we must change the conditions that allow these problems to exist and flourish.

Economic issues with social consequences

Most crimes in our community are committed for economic reasons. So, what do we do? We build more jails.

We cannot build enough jails to solve the crime problem. What we must do is transform the *poor* economic environment that feeds the proliferation of crime into a *productive* economic environment that is creating jobs and lowering the unemployment rate, which will lower the crime rate. People who are employed typically do not commit crimes.

Or consider the challenge of failing schools. While I believe we should improve our school infrastructures and pay our teachers a fair salary for their skills, I don't believe that these things alone will solve the problem of failing schools. At the core of failing schools are our children—more specifically, the poor economic environments in which they live. How can we expect children to study and learn when they are hungry, home alone, and live in environments infested with drugs and crime, and in houses with no heat in the winter and no air conditioning in the summer?

And what about the challenge of working to eliminate police brutality in our communities? Should we continue to work on this challenge? Absolutely! But we should also understand that even if we awaken tomorrow and there are no more deaths at the hands of white police officers, there will still be deaths at the hands of other blacks in our communities.

My point is simple: while these issues, on the surface, appear to be social in nature, they are actually *economic issues with social consequences*, and solving any one of them will not transform the economics of the African-American community. These issues do not exist in communities where there is a thriving economy.

Definitions and context

This book has a very urgent and specific focus: converting our political power to economic power.

Therefore, I believe it is imperative to define a few terms, so that you can understand, with clarity and expediency, the message of this book, and begin to develop appropriate strategies and behaviors directed at meeting this Historical Challenge.

Political Power

The essence of our political power as African-Americans is that we're controlling a lot of money. As elected and appointed black officials, we either control or influence how trillions of public dollars are spent; we spend millions of dollars as executives and managers of major corporations; and as black consumers, we spend more than $1.1 trillion a year.

Economic Power (Silver Rights)

We will become economically empowered when we spend the money we own or control (our political power) with the businesses in our communities that reinvest in our communities.

The Historical Challenge (Converting Political Power to Economic Power)

As African-American professionals, elected and appointed officials, and consumers, we're controlling a lot of money—but that money is not being used in ways that change the masses of black people's economic reality. It's not being used in ways where it's solving our social problems, our employment and education problems, our crime problems, our health and housing problems. To convert our political power to economic power, we must start spending the money we own or control with the businesses in our communities that reinvest in our communities. To make this conversion possible, we must build the black business class.

Wealth

When we go to Scripture, we find that Deuteronomy 8:18 reads, "And you shall remember the LORD your God, for it is He who gives you power to get wealth [. . .]." So let's be clear: we acquire wealth—we don't create it. The Lord has already created all of the wealth that exists. So we have to go out and get it, and we get it through an exchange process.

This wealth that I speak of is not the wealth that they speak of on Wall Street—the kind that the more you get, the more you want. I'm speaking of the wealth that must exist on Main Street—the kind of wealth that allows you to provide for your family and still have excess capital to invest in your community.

Wall Street wealth is usually seen as something individualized, but Main Street wealth has a collective value. It is derived from a people converting political power to economic power with the goal of changing the economic reality of our communities and the lives of the people who reside in those communities. The key to achieving collective wealth in the African-American community is the growth of the black business class.

The urgent need to refocus our efforts

I believe people are crying out for change. And they're looking for something to be a part of—to be part of that change.

With young black men across America dying at the hands of white police officers, there's a movement that people are trying to rally around, and people are saying that this is the new Civil Rights Movement.

Unfortunately, there is no effective leadership to direct the people. There is no effective leadership articulating the fact that these social and civil crises are not the actual problem. These crises are only *symptoms* of the problem, which is our lack of economic power as African-Americans.

When we address only the symptoms, we lose sight of the real problem—and we don't *solve* the real problem.

We certainly need to continue to fight these social and civil crises wherever we may find them, but we also need to be conscious that that fight is going to exist as long as capitalism exists. Capitalism has great benefits, allowing people to acquire wealth, but it also has an evil side—because in order for capitalism to exist, there has to be a poor class and there has to be a rich class.

I understand why people are rallying around this issue. Any single thing that you can jump on that you think is going to be a movement, to solve all these other issues—you want to be a part of that. For the last fifty years, there has not been a movement. People today, especially the younger generation, want to jump on something that suggests they are doing their part to bring about change. It's great that they're doing something, but what they are doing is not going to generate the changes that are required to overcome our twenty-first-century Historical Challenge.

The reason that we haven't progressed towards meeting our Historical Challenge is that we're out here putting out fires, rather than dealing with what is *causing* these fires. Every time we put one fire out here, another fire erupts over there. We're not dealing with the cause of the fires; we're not dealing with the Historical Challenge. Only when we focus on the Historical Challenge will we start to see a fundamental change in the economic condition of our people.

We had all kinds of issues during the Historical Challenge of slavery. For example, we didn't have access to education during slavery. The reason we weren't getting education is that we were slaves; slaves weren't allowed to be educated. But rather than focusing on the single issue "we're not allowed to be educated," we focused on what was creating the problem: slavery, and the laws that governed slavery.

The Civil Rights Movement was the same. Ultimately we looked at the Constitution and said that constitutionally, this is what must be done for us to overcome the Historical Challenge of Jim Crow and the denial of our civil rights. We could have dealt with each issue individually, but we never would have solved the bigger problem.

The American Dream

For the last fifty years, we've been dealing with individual symptoms, but now we've got to deal with the Historical Challenge: taking our political power and converting it to economic power.

Money gives you power to access the American Dream. As it is written in Ecclesiastes 10:19, "A feast is made for laughter, and wine makes merry; but money answers everything."

America is a capitalistic country. Capital is king. Good, bad, or ugly, that's what it is. And if we're going to change the economic reality of our people, then we've got to use our political power and convert it to economic power. That's what will change the condition of our poor and solve the problems in our communities.

While we will never eliminate poverty, we want to move as many people as possible out of poverty and up to the middle class, and ultimately make the middle class larger. Because in the middle class, you may not be wealthy, but you are able to provide for your family and enjoy more of the American Dream.

Understanding the historical context of the challenge

The Fifteenth Amendment to the United States Constitution, ratified on February 3, 1870, prohibits the federal and state governments from denying a citizen the right to vote based on that citizen's "race, color, or previous condition of servitude."

Despite its passage in 1870, most black voters in the South remained disenfranchised by the United States Supreme Court's narrow interpretation of this Amendment, and by the state constitutions and state laws incorporating such obstacles as poll taxes and discriminatory literacy tests.

However, our people refused to remain second-class citizens. African-Americans mounted the most powerful resistance movement of the twentieth century—the Civil Rights Movement—forcing Congress to pass the Civil Rights Act of 1964 and the Voting Rights Act of 1965.

The Civil Rights Act of 1964

The Civil Rights Act of 1964 outlawed discrimination based on race, color, religion, sex, or national origin. It ended unequal application of voter registration requirements, and prohibited racial segregation in schools, at the workplace, and by facilities that served the general public, known as "public accommodations." It is sometimes referred to as the Accommodation Act, or the Public Accommodation Act.

The Civil Rights Act ushered in black professionals at all levels of government and in Corporate America, putting them in control of money or in charge of decisions that impacted how money was spent. It allowed us to create the black professional class that we now have.

Prior to the Civil Rights Act, we didn't have that professional class because we weren't operating in those disciplines. And now we operate in those disciplines. We head up corporations, we're CEOs, and we lead Head Starts, community health care clinics, and universities. All of this contributes to our political power.

The Voting Rights Act of 1965

The Voting Rights Act of 1965 was designed to enforce the voting rights guaranteed by the Fourteenth and Fifteenth Amendments to the United States Constitution. This Act provided federal oversight of elections in discriminatory jurisdictions, banned literacy tests and similar discriminatory devices, and created legal remedies for people affected by voting discrimination.

The Voting Rights Act of 1965 was critical to the political empowerment of African-Americans. Once African-Americans were able to exercise their constitutional rights to vote, they went to the polls in great numbers to elect blacks as mayors in major cities, to Congress, and to other elected offices. Today this manifestation of our political power has placed trillions of public dollars under the control of African-Americans in cities, counties, and public bodies all across America.

A Luta Continua: The Struggle Continues

So black professionals are controlling political power (money) in corporations, and black elected officials are controlling political power (money) in government, as the direct result of the Civil Rights Act of 1964 and the Voting Rights Act of 1965. Those two legislations actually created two important pillars of political power, which has also led to a growth in African-American consumers' buying power.

Yet here in the twenty-first century, our struggle continues. Today we have much more political power, yet we lack the economic power to transform our communities and solve systemic problems.

Those willing to take on today's Historical Challenge must not view it as a thoughtless process to embark on, but as a progression rising out of two centuries of labor without wages, suffering through injustice, countless deaths, and shameful humiliation from two previous Historical Challenges.

Note that our Historical Challenges have occurred in this progression. The Civil Rights Movement could not have taken place without the abolition movement. And without the Civil Rights Movement, we would not have our current political power, which we now must convert to economic power. Many, if not all, of the accomplishments that we enjoy today—more doctors, lawyers, professionals, college graduates, mayors, and other elected officials—can be attributed to the previous generations' meeting their Historical Challenges.

The nineteenth-century challenge to defeat slavery and win abolition achieved our human rights and individual power.

The twentieth-century challenge to defeat Jim Crow and the denial of our constitutional rights achieved our civil rights and political power.

And now, we face the twenty-first-century challenge to defeat our economic problems and the resulting social problems, and achieve our Silver Rights—our economic power.

As a people, we have a history of fighting against things, but this twenty-first-century challenge requires us to fight for something.

The nineteenth- and twentieth-century Historical Challenges had to do with fighting against overt forms of slavery and discrimination. Those two challenges were resistance struggles. We were resisting powers that were being exerted on us. And the enemy, so to speak, was overt: we could see it.

Those struggles are different from where we find ourselves today. Now, we can't see the enemy—because in essence, the enemy is us.

We control all of this political power, and we have $1.1 trillion of buying power—yet our communities are deteriorating.

Our schools are deteriorating. Crime is at an all-time high. Unemployment is at an all-time high.

How can we have so much buying power and so much political power, yet all of these problems continue to exist in our communities? It's simple: because we haven't converted our political power to economic power, and we haven't empowered the people to take what they have and use it to change their own lives. Meanwhile other communities, such as the Asian and Hispanic communities, have solved these problems, because they understand the concept of economic problems with social consequences. They know there can be no economic transformation of a community without a strong and thriving business class.

We already have what it takes to win.

The first step in acquiring economic power is for African-Americans to realize that we already possess the core ingredients for acquiring wealth. These core ingredients are:

1. Our annual buying power of $1.1 trillion.

2. The billions of public dollars that African-Americans control in city governments and public entities—dollars that can be directed to black-owned businesses, if blacks occupying seats of power in these governments and entities choose to do so. Using political power to effect change is not self-serving when it is done for its intended purpose: to improve the lives

of those you represent. Power must never be separated from responsibility.

We no longer have a logical reason to blame others for the condition we find ourselves in. While others can and must help, the buck stops with us.

We must start the march toward Economic Empowerment ourselves.

Communities grow when people invest in them. We should not expect others to come into our communities and be the primary investors in our communities. That is our responsibility, and we must do it. We must start the march towards Silver Rights ourselves.

Our predecessors created opportunities for economic power like never before, and now we must take advantage of these opportunities, both individually and collectively as a community. We must start making tough decisions and taking responsibility for how we spend our dollars.

As the great African-American writer Paul Robeson, Jr., wrote, "We played a major role in growing America from a small colonial outpost to the greatest industrial giant the world has ever known. We don't have to argue about our ability to grow wealth. We have made everyone else rich, some filthy rich. Isn't it time that we finally make our efforts productive for ourselves?"

Creating this new economy in our communities through a strong business class will require us to engage the situation with the same level of passion and determination that was evident during the Civil Rights Movement.

No other group has endured what African-Americans have endured in America.

Each generation is charged with the responsibility of facing the challenges of its times. Our fathers and forefathers did it. First they faced the wrath of slavery and defeated it. Then they faced the denial of civil rights and defeated it. These two struggles created what we enjoy today: political power. Our generation's responsibility is to convert that political power to economic power.

In fact, it is these Historical Challenges that separate us from others who dare suggest that their struggle is just like ours. Nothing is further from the truth. No other group of people has had to wage the struggles that we have had to wage, and still wage, in America.

Don't let people, even some of our so-called black leaders, tell you that other groups' struggles are the same as those of our fathers and forefathers. That is an insult to them—an insult to Fannie Lou Hammer, Frederick Douglass, Medgar Evers, Dr. Martin Luther King, Jr., Malcolm X, Harriet Tubman, and so many others.

Instead, let us rise to the challenge of our unique responsibility.

Dr. Martin Luther King, Jr., said, "We must now develop economic parity. No ethnic group in America has ever gained equality in America without first achieving economic parity."

Dr. King made this declaration in November 1967, the night Carl Stokes was elected mayor of Cleveland and became the first African-American mayor of a major U.S. city. Dr. King was acknowledging our political power, while also emphasizing that we had more work to do and another Historical Challenge to overcome.

How do we take the power derived from the passages of the Civil Rights Act of 1964 and the Voting Rights Act of 1965, and convert that to economic power?

We must build the black business class.

The black business class is an absolutely critical component in the Silver Rights equation because this business class, not government, forms the foundation for community reinvestment. Government must create the climate, conditions, and infrastructure for business opportunity, but business investment must come from individuals—namely, the black business class.

There is a reason why the white business class is the most influential force in the white community: it creates jobs and advances economic development. The white political leader takes his directions from the white business class.

However, in the African-American community, it is the black political leader who is in control, while the black business class is virtually nonexistent. This must change. Our destiny and the economic transformation of our community are tied to the growth of the black business class.

Growing minority-owned businesses is crucial for America's economic success in the twenty-first century, according to a joint report issued by The Milken Institute and the Minority Business Development Agency:

• Entrepreneurs fuel the American economy; they are its most important source of jobs, income, and wealth acquisition.

• Minorities are forming businesses at a much faster rate than their non-minority counterparts.

• Minority businesses tend to create more jobs for minorities.

• As minorities grow to comprise a larger percentage of the American population, their success—or failure—will have a profound effect on the entire American economy.

The report further states:

The future of the nation's economic growth depends upon the inclusion of minority-owned businesses and the minority business workforce, and access to capital for minority-owned businesses is absolutely essential for the healthy development of this growing sector of American business.

This point is especially urgent for black businesses. Other than government, black businesses are the greatest job creator for African-Americans. And when you consider the current unemployment rate among African-Americans, particularly African-American men, growing the black business class is of critical importance.

Creating economic power requires investment and ownership, not just spending.

African-Americans' annual buying power increased exponentially in the twenty-first century to $1.1 trillion, yet we repeatedly make poor choices on where, how, with whom, and on what we spend our money.

It is a fact that, as a community, we save or invest only three percent of our annual income, and spend almost all of it outside our own communities. We must examine the economic consequences of what I believe to be irresponsible spending choices that we African-Americans make with our money.

Just look at the spending habits of African-Americans as reported by Target Market News in its 16th edition of *The Buying Power of Black America*:

- Apparel Products and Services, $29 Billion
- Appliances, $2 Billion
- Alcoholic Beverages, $3 Billion
- Non-Alcoholic Beverages, $2.8 Billion
- Books, $321 Million
- New and Used Autos, $29.1 Billion
- Computers, $3.6 Billion
- Consumer Electronics, $6.1 Billion
- Education, $7.5 Billion
- Entertainment, $3.1 Billion
- Food, $65 Billion
- Health Care, $23.6 Billion
- Household Furnishings and Equipment, $16.5 Billion
- Housing and Related Charges, $203.8 Billion
- Insurance, $21.3 Billion
- Media, $8.8 Billion
- Personal and Professional Services, $4.1 Billion

- Personal Care Products and Services, $7.4 Billion
- Telephone Services, $18.6 Billion
- Tobacco Products, $3.3 Billion
- Transportation, Travel and Lodging, $6 Billion

Now look at these numbers carefully. They tell an important story. What is evident is that ninety percent of the money that African-Americans earn is spent on products and services that do not support Economic Empowerment or wealth accumulation. For instance, we invest four times the amount of money in cars, which quickly lose value, as we invest in education, which builds a foundation for future wealth acquisition.

Also, most of these products and services are acquired outside of the black community. This tells me that our money is flying out of our hands and into the hands of others, primarily those who live outside of our communities. The reality is that many of the products African-Americans purchase *must* be purchased outside of our own communities—simply because we do not have the capacity to produce them.

We need to build and support a thriving business class.

It is imperative that we establish the kinds of businesses that can provide many of the products and services that we currently purchase elsewhere.

And, once established, we must support these businesses by purchasing products and services from them. We need to build and support a thriving business class. These are critical pieces to plugging the holes in the African-American Economic Empowerment equation. We must come to understand that, when our money is not retained in our communities, our communities then lack the necessary investment dollars to be self-sustaining, resulting in economic and social instability that ultimately promote decay. Conversely, when dollars are reinvested in the community, stability is created and decay is halted.

I view wealth as a function of ownership or net assets (stocks, bonds, real estate, and businesses)—and out of all of these assets, business ownership is the most important. Business ownership forms the foundation for an economy, which allows for the circulation of money. As money circulates, jobs are created, procurement of other products and services from other businesses occurs, and profits are generated for savings and reinvestment back into the community.

Turning the dollar over within the community

If you spend your dollars at a black-owned store in your neighborhood, the store owner then spends those dollars at a black-owned printing company, whose owner in turn puts those dollars into a black-owned bank that holds mortgages for homeowners in the neighborhood. Thus, African-Americans are allowing their dollars to circulate within the black community.

In general, a dollar should circulate about eight to ten times before it leaves a community in order for the community to gain the full effect of its value. The longer capital (the dollar) remains in the community, the greater the opportunity for that capital to grow an economy and build stability, helping to solve the problems our communities are facing.

The real building blocks in this scenario are the people who make the smart decisions to save and invest in their community.

- The black elected or appointed leader who finds a way to get black businesses involved in the procurement process

- The printer who puts his or her money into savings

- The bank owner who chooses to lend money to the homeowner

- The homeowner who chooses to invest in his home

- The businessmen who run small businesses and create jobs in their own community

These are the key players in the Silver Rights Movement. The longer their dollar stays in their community, the greater the opportunity for their community to build wealth, or gain Silver Rights.

Business ownership alone is not enough. The category and capacity of the businesses are also key.

The principal component for establishing and retaining capital within a community is business ownership. Recently released economic statistics on the number of minority-owned businesses show that they are increasing substantially faster than the national average. But business ownership by itself is not enough, and the numbers bear this out.

According to the most recent Economic Census SBO (Survey of Business Owners), African-Americans, Hispanics, and Asians own roughly the same number of businesses but with very different results.

- Businesses owned by Asians, who make up 5 percent of the U.S. population, generate about $506 billion in annual sales revenues.

- Businesses owned by Hispanics, who make up 17 percent of the population, generate about $351 billion in annual sales revenues.

- Businesses owned by African-Americans, who makes up 13 percent of the population, generate about $136 billion in annual sales revenues.

Minority ownership	Number/businesses	Annual sales	Adult population
Black	1.9 million	$136 billion	26.4 million
Hispanic	2.3 million	$351 billion	30 million
Asian	1.5 million	$506 billion	10 million

So, Hispanic- and Asian-owned businesses generate two-and-a-half times to almost four times the total annual sales revenues generated by black-owned businesses. How can this be possible, especially when the $1.1 trillion annual buying power of African-Americans is almost twice that of Asians or Hispanics?

One answer to this question is that the current class and capacity of African-American-owned businesses are inadequate to create the kind of economy that is sufficient to generate wealth in the twenty-first century.

For instance, Hispanics had more construction companies and Asians had more professional service companies compared to African-Americans, who had more health care and social assistance companies.

Therefore, African-Americans must increase the number and types of black-owned businesses, as well as build the capacity of current businesses to generate more revenue.

Other successes in the Asian and Hispanic business communities suggest additional ideas that may be relevant to building the black business class.

Taking consistent action

Hispanics in America are setting the example for taking consistent and energetic action to build their business class: they opened new businesses about ten times faster than the entire U.S. population from 1990 through 2012. During those twenty-two years, their rate of new business growth exceeded the total population growth of Hispanics in America. Hispanics weren't stopped by language barriers, lack of education, low socioeconomic status, or other obstacles, and they continued to open new businesses during the recession.

Strengthening families through business ownership

Many Asian and Hispanic small businesses are family businesses that strengthen their nuclear and extended families by providing jobs. Being family brings special trust and loyalty to the employer-employee relationship, and family employees have a sense of personal investment and commitment to the business's success. The family members share the responsibilities as well as the benefits of owning the business. All of these factors create positive effects, not only within the family, but in the community as well.

Focusing on success

Asian small businesses have found ways to thrive economically without pitting themselves in direct competition against each other. One way they do so is through ethnic niches. For instance, Asian Indians dominate the hotels and lodgings sector; Vietnamese focus on fishing and hunting categories; and Koreans are more concentrated in retail apparel and accessories. The concept of ethnic niches may not be directly applicable in the African-American community. What is relevant, however, is the fact that Asian businesses can succeed without having to drive other Asians out of business. This mindset put into practice can consistently lead to Economic Empowerment for African-Americans, for both the individual and the community.

Bringing people together

In addition to circulating dollars within the community, businesses are physical spaces or gathering places for people to share networking, social support, and other connections that strengthen individuals and communities. Whether the economy is up or down, the solidarity that people find in such gathering places helps lift a community up, and inspires new ideas and actions.

This kind of social empowerment is not unique to Asian and Hispanic neighborhoods. It was strong in African-American neighborhoods throughout our previous Historical Challenges, and remains true today in barber shops, beauty salons, groceries, and other business located in black neighborhoods. African-Americans can increase their social empowerment by continuing to build the black business class in their communities.

We must do more than review history. We must plot the course to create history.

Our fathers and forefathers waged two historical battles before us: the battles for abolition and civil rights. While they certainly want us to acknowledge their struggles, they don't want us to re-fight the battles that they've already won. They want us to face the Historical Challenge that we now have the responsibility for addressing.

In order for African-Americans to take what we possess and use it for our economic advantage, we must first understand our past. The courageous African-American men and women of the nineteenth and twentieth centuries faced far more difficult challenges than the ones we face today. Drawing on their spirit and resiliency, as I will do in *Part II: Understanding Our Historical Challenge*, we can strengthen our resolve to meet the Economic Empowerment challenge of our generation.

We must also awaken the new leaders of this generation to take on their historic responsibility and charge them with the task of launching this twenty-first-century movement for Economic Empowerment.

Great leaders interpret and articulate the conditions and Historical Challenges of their people, and provide a strategy for meeting those challenges. These new leaders are members of the emerging black business class, primarily those high-level managers whose business knowledge and expertise gained in Corporate America give them the best chance at entrepreneurial success. Their success will lead to economic success for us all.

In *Part III: Overcoming Our Historical Challenge*, you will meet some of these leaders. You will also discover your individual calling: the key roles you can play as we meet our Historical Challenge with a twenty-first-century strategy.

Economic challenges demand economic solutions.

Attaining political power was never meant to be an end; it was only intended as a means to an end.

Economic power is the highest expression of political power, and acquiring it is the next logical step when you consider African-Americans' historical struggles in America. We must embrace the Historical Challenge of converting political power to economic power. Our time is now.

PART II:

Understanding Our Historical Challenge

Those who cannot remember the past are condemned to repeat it.

—George Santayana

The past can and must be a compass to guide our collective actions, while also serving as a barometer to measure nation-building progress.

—Mutumwa Dziva Mawere

Sayings like these are often repeated. Unfortunately, it appears African-Americans today have not learned the lessons they convey. But it is my desire that we forge an understanding and appreciation of those men and women who came before us and who fought hard to earn the civil liberties, rights, and opportunities that we now enjoy.

We are no longer fighting to free ourselves from atrocious and inhumane conditions of physical slavery, nor are we fighting for our civil rights. Our ancestors waged and won those battles over the last two centuries, and they do not require us to refight them. Thanks to them, we have the political power to transform our economic conditions. Our next great battle is to convert this political power to economic power.

Today we require leadership with the capacity to wake the people up and unite us in a movement that will focus our attention, energy, and resources on this twenty-first-century Historical Challenge. We cannot afford leadership that will poison our efforts with old, contaminated thoughts based on old challenges. If you are afraid to stand up today for what is right and what is needed by our people, then you are not an effective leader; you are simply an opportunist looking for an opportunity. Those who are afraid will never be able to provide appropriate and effective leadership.

The African-American leadership of the twenty-first century must take to heart the lessons from black leaders of the past, not only in what they were fighting for, but also *how they fought—and how they succeeded*. I urge African-Americans to examine our history closely, because it has the power to teach, inspire, and empower us to achieve greatness.

Overcoming our new Historical Challenge will require us to create a balance between tradition and innovation. We must take the examples of sacrifice and collective struggle demonstrated by our forebears, and combine them with innovations in technology and social media to direct the people's efforts towards our mission of converting political power to economic power.

Our Nineteenth-Century Historical Challenge: Slavery and the Abolition Movement

Resistance movements are byproducts of an oppressed people's discontentment with their conditions. Determined leaders who hear the call for service and sacrifice guide the people through challenges to victory. These leaders are seasoned by the trials and tribulations of their struggles and fueled by a determination to break the stronghold of an unjust and merciless system.

The abolition movement and its leaders of the nineteenth century embodied those characteristics. These heroes' efforts should be studied, remembered, appreciated, and most of all—emulated.

The beginning of legalized enslavement

African-American recorded roots of slavery in North America can be traced back to the seventeenth-century British colonists of Jamestown, Virginia, where the first Africans were brought as forced laborers in 1619. They were called "indentured servants" because they could become free after fulfilling their contractual obligations. Initially, there were no laws permitting slavery, but indentured servitude was widely practiced. In 1641, Massachusetts legalized the enslavement of Africans. That set off a domino effect, with laws legalizing and legitimizing the transformation of indentured servants into African slaves sweeping among the American colonies.

The more Africans resisted these acts, the greater was the oppression to limit their freedoms. In 1680, Virginia passed the Act for Preventing Negro Insurrection, prohibiting blacks from possessing anything that could be used as a weapon, such as farm tools and sticks. Runaway slaves, if captured and found to have resisted, could be and oftentimes were put to death.

Seizing opportunities

Even as they were disembarking from the slave ships, nursing their wounds from the torturous trek across the Atlantic, African-Americans understood the power of wealth and money. They saw it in the greedy eyes of their white buyers. They saw it in the value of the land they worked and in the crops they wrestled from the soil. Whenever possible, they made use of that knowledge.

"Beginning in the 1600s, Africans in America, slave and free, seized every opportunity to develop enterprises and participate as businesspeople in the commercial life of a developing new nation," wrote Juliet E.K. Walker in *The History of Black Business in America*.

These enslaved men and women knew that in a better world, they would be free to strike out on their own, to stake a claim, raise a crop, and take it to the market. They knew those dollars they saw passing through white hands would be just as valuable in their own hands. Even then, our people had a keen understanding of Economic Empowerment. But the pressing issue of slavery and a destiny with Jim Crow delayed their hopes of being full participants in the American Dream.

Slaves cultivated tobacco, cotton, and rice on their own provision grounds, and sold their surpluses to each other, to their owners, and at public markets. Through the practice of "hiring their own time," slaves could earn money in a variety of endeavors. Thus slaves and free blacks earned money as craftsmen, tailors, barbers, carpenters, carriage makers, boat navigators, and construction workers; slave women earned money as dressmakers, hairdressers, bakers, cooks, laundresses, and in agricultural work.

Many slaves saved their earnings to buy their freedom and the freedom of family members and friends. Free blacks used their profits to purchase others' freedom and to expand their businesses. While they quickly grasped the value of property and labor, and did all they could to turn this knowledge to their advantage, they were also cruelly reminded of the restrictions placed upon them. A slave had no control over real commerce. The law did not allow it.

The Revolutionary War

Blacks, both freed in the North and enslaved in the South, continued to resist during this first one hundred years of slavery. Blacks and anti-slavery supporters demanded that colonial governors and legislators release the slaves and return them to Africa. Ironically, blacks used the same language of freedom, equality, and justice in their petitions as white colonists used in their struggle to free themselves from the British.

Blacks even fought and died in America's first war for independence. In fact, the first person to die in the American Revolution was a black former slave, Crispus Attucks, in the 1770 Boston Massacre.

While all of America fought for freedom from the British, we were fighting for our freedom from slavery. Thousands of blacks, both free and slave, fought in the Revolutionary War. We were committed to fighting on the side that would guarantee the freedom we desired. Both the British and the Americans promised freedom to slaves who enlisted in their armies, but the majority of blacks joined the American side.

At the end of the war, we expected America's leaders to be more sensitive to our cause, given that we had just engaged in a war, fighting for freedom alongside them. However, this was not to be. Some slaves were granted their freedom as promised, but the majority of black soldiers who had fought for American independence were relegated to the same status they had held before the war.

White America became "the land of the free and the home of the brave," but for blacks it remained the land of slaves, as America reneged on its promise and intensified its system of slavery.

The new Constitution regarded slaves as three-fifths of a human, insuring that political power would remain in the possession of whites. As a result of this three-fifths status, slaves were not counted as citizens, and therefore were unable to benefit from the newfound freedom being enjoyed by white Americans.

But our people were not deterred by America's failure to acknowledge the right of all men to be free. The denial of freedom only served to escalate the black resistance movement through organized efforts and written protests. Famed black astronomer, farmer, and surveyor Benjamin Banneker had these words to say to Thomas Jefferson, the drafter of the Declaration of Independence, in his letter of 1791:

> Sir, how pitiable it is to reflect, that although you were so fully convinced of the benevolence of the Father of mankind, and of his equal and impartial distribution of these rights and privileges which he hath conferred upon them, that you should at the same time counteract his mercies, in detaining by fraud

and violence so numerous a part of my brethren under groaning captivity and cruel oppression; that you should at the same time be found guilty of that most criminal act which you professedly detested in others with respect to yourselves.

The right to be in America

The American Colonization Society (ACS) organized in 1816. The ACS, consisting mainly of southern slaveholders and prominent white clergy and politicians, helped to establish Liberia, a colony in Africa, to take free people of color away from the United States. Led by U.S. President James Monroe, the ACS intended to drive free Africans from the North out of America, and to prevent them from rising up in revolt against slavery.

Freed blacks saw colonization as a threat to their ability to remain in America. This colonization movement was an impetus for an organized black abolitionist movement. Between 1817 and 1819, mass meetings were held condemning colonization, protests that set the tone for the resistance movement of the nineteenth century. In meetings at homes, churches, and other locations across the North, African-Americans expressed their anger and dissatisfaction with those seeking to remove them from America. They affirmed their identity, and reminded whites that they had helped create this new republic and put their lives on the line for the revolutionary cause. They were claiming rights to be in America. Leaving was not an option.

America's freed black population had ballooned to more than 300,000 by 1830 (up from 60,000 in 1790), mostly in the North. The increase in numbers created social tensions between blacks and whites. Freed blacks were now competing for the same jobs as whites. Blacks were buying businesses, including livery coach and delivery services, general and grocery stores, and dining and music establishments. They were purchasing real estate and sending their children to the same schools as whites, at least in the North.

To circumvent this growing empowerment of blacks, whites began to enact local laws. In an effort to curtail the impacts of those discriminatory changes, blacks begin to organize on a massive scale, planning, strategizing, and plotting courses of actions. The first National Negro Convention was held in Philadelphia in 1830, when blacks defiantly called for a violent overthrow of the slave system, rebelled against oppression, and promoted self-reliance. Some even spoke of voluntary emigration from the United States. The small delegation of leaders at the National Negro Convention drafted strong resolutions supporting emigration to Canada rather than to Liberia.

The American Anti-Slavery Society

Prior to 1833, anti-slavery efforts were waged in a very sporadic fashion with little or no focus. However, December 1833 marked the founding convention of the American Anti-Slavery Society

(AASS), an organized movement to abolish slavery. The Philadelphia meeting included prominent African-American reformers such as James G. Barbadoes, a Boston clothier and barber; James McCrummill, a barber and dentist; and Robert Purvis, a young anti-slavery activist who was the first African-American to serve as President of the AASS (1845-1850). The AASS also included whites, mostly clergymen from Quaker and Protestant churches, representing eleven states—and William Lloyd Garrison, who became the most recognized and influential white abolitionist in American history.

William Lloyd Garrison had embraced the colonization philosophy for the gradual elimination of slavery, but after working with African-Americans in Baltimore and Philadelphia, he discarded those views and advocated immediate elimination of slavery. Garrison's support for immediate abolition added momentum to the anti-slavery movement and led other white reformers to join black abolitionists. This redirected the abolition movement in America.

The American Anti-Slavery Society Declaration of Sentiments, written by Garrison and adopted on the last day of the founding convention, was the racially diverse group's consensus on the goals and strategies for the anti-slavery movement. It denounced slavery and included an immediate call for its end without compensation for slave owners.

The Declaration of Sentiments also condemned the back-to-Africa efforts of the ACS, which the AASS saw as propaganda and a slaveholders' scheme for the continuation of slavery in the United States.

Barely three years into the abolition movement, the AASS boasted more than five hundred chapters across the North. Black and white leaders were now working together, guided by moral reform, and replacing aggression and confrontation with public appeals and speeches. The article in the AASS Declaration of Sentiments rejected violence and the use of force, trusting instead in the "overthrow of prejudice by the power of love and the abolition of slavery by the spirit of repentance."

Black abolitionists pursue the broader vision

The black leadership realized that the non-aggressive approach was not working. The number of slaves was increasing each year. Race relations were strained to the limit. Voting rights in the North were being lost, and there was an increase in the kidnapping of fugitive slaves, free blacks, and children.

Black abolitionists and former slaves such as Frederick Douglass also concluded that there was too great a difference in the approaches of white and black abolition leadership. Douglass had been a very close confidant of William Lloyd Garrison, but now found himself in the forefront of a new phase of the abolition movement. Douglass believed that freedom was not something that was given, but fought for. White abolitionists saw their movement only as an instrument for eradicating slavery in the

South, while black abolitionists had a much broader vision that included eradicating the political, economic, and social ills that were also by-products of racism in the North.

Independence from white abolitionists ushered in a new generation of African-American leadership in the 1840s. Frederick Douglass, Samuel Ringgold, Martin R. Delany, Jermain W. Loguen, and James Smith were among those who provided leadership during this critical time. Unlike previous leaders, who were part of an older black elite class of educated and wealthy businessmen, these new leaders were younger and had made their way to the abolition movement by way of the plantation and hands-on, direct anti-slavery efforts.

This new leadership also included women: Sojourner Truth, Sarah Parker Remond, Harriet Tubman, and others who were journalists, lecturers, and authors. Truth, a tall woman of great dignity and dedication, was once threatened at a speaking engagement by slavery supporters who vowed to burn down the building. She boldly responded, "Then I will speak upon the ashes."

The Dred Scott decision in 1856

With the advent of the Mexican War, slavery was expanding in the West. The government enacted laws that strengthened the position of slave owners, even though the division between pro- and anti-slavery factions was escalating. The Dred Scott decision, in which the United States Supreme Court declared that the U.S. territories could not prohibit slavery and that free blacks did not have constitutional rights, is said to have been one of the key events leading up to the Civil War.

Born a slave in Virginia at the turn of the nineteenth century, Dred Scott was later taken by his master to Illinois and then Minnesota. Once in free territory, Scott filed a lawsuit claiming that his residency in these free territories should result in freedom for him and his family. Many slaves before him had successfully claimed such rights. However, times were changing.

When the U.S. Supreme Court in 1856 denied Scott's appeal from the state court, Chief Supreme Court Justice Roger B. Taney, in the 7-2 decision, said blacks "had no rights which the white man was bound to respect." The highest court in the land basically said the Founding Fathers did not view blacks as citizens when they drafted the Constitution.

Frederick Douglass led the challenge against the decision. He and others felt they had almost exhausted all manner of legal, political, and other passive resistance. While speaking to the American Abolitionist Society (AAS) a few months later, Douglass stated:

> The limits of tyrants are prescribed by the endurance of those whom they oppress [. . .]. If we ever get free from the oppressions and wrongs heaped upon us, we must pay for their re-

moval. We must do this by labor, by suffering, by sacrifice, and if needs be, by our lives and the lives of others.

Support from others: the raid on Harpers Ferry

In 1859, John Brown, a militant white abolitionist, seized a federal arsenal in Harpers Ferry, West Virginia, intending to arm runaway slaves. John Brown's raid on Harpers Ferry changed the course of American history and represented yet another turning point in the abolition movement. Even though Brown failed, the raid focused the nation's attention on the issue of slavery.

In the wake of Brown's trial and execution, blacks elevated him to the status of hero and martyr. He represented a fusion of militant abolitionism with America's revolutionary heritage. It is said that Brown lived his life for black freedom but surrendered it for white sin.

The Harpers Ferry raid prompted a display of interracial unity not observed during the anti-slavery movement since the early days of William Lloyd Garrison. The memorial ceremonies that followed Brown's execution brought thousands of whites and blacks together, united in their veneration of Brown and his actions.

For blacks, the Harpers Ferry raid signaled slavery's imminent demise. The raid ignited a renewed call for rebellion and armed revolt against the South.

The Civil War's three perspectives: North, South, and African-American

Civil War broke out in April 1861 when Confederate troops attacked Union troops at Fort Sumter in South Carolina. Most Northern whites rallied to defend the Constitution and preserve the Union. Southern whites fought for independence to guarantee states' rights, preserve a way of life, and secure a system of slavery. Blacks understood the war very differently from either Northern or Southern whites. For blacks, it was the beginning of the end of slavery, and a huge test in their bid for freedom.

Frederick Douglass, like so many other black leaders, saw the war and black participation as a means of ending slavery and ensuring full citizenship for blacks. In 1863, in the publication entitled *Men of Color, To Arms*, Douglass called on blacks to join the fight for their liberty:

> I urge you to fly to arms and smite with death the power that would bury the government and your liberty in the same hopeless grave [. . .]. The chance is now given you to end in a day that bondage of centuries, and to rise in one bound from social degradation to the plane of common equality with all other varieties of men.

Stand ready "as Minute Men, to respond when the slave calls."

Some blacks vigorously opposed the war and decided to withhold their approval until the destruction of slavery became the war's principal aim. Religious leaders declared that blacks had no business fighting for a country that oppressed them, and the black press reminded its readers that their first responsibility was to the slave. The *Weekly Anglo-African New York*, the most influential black paper of the era, counseled blacks to denounce the government but to organize, drill, and stand ready "as Minute Men, to respond when the slave calls."

Some blacks rushed to enlist in the Union Army after the attack on Fort Sumter, believing that national war aims would certainly include emancipation. But the more than 8,500 men who had joined black volunteer militia units by the fall of 1861 were rejected for military service by the federal government. Wounded by the rejection and angered by official indifference to their patriotism and aspirations, most blacks resolved to save their "labors for the slave and the slave alone," and left the government to fend for itself.

Lincoln's military strategy

Facing the prospect of a prolonged war with appalling Union casualties, Northern leaders began to reexamine the use of black troops. More importantly, Lincoln concluded that a Union victory depended upon eliminating one of the South's most valuable assets—its slave labor population—through emancipation.

The Emancipation Proclamation, issued by President Abraham Lincoln on Monday, September 22, 1862, declared all slaves to be freed. Lincoln called together his Cabinet and expressed to them the following: "I have, as you are aware, thought a great deal about the relation of this war to slavery." He told them that, since the war started, he had believed that the Union cause eventually would be linked to emancipation.

The Emancipation Proclamation was distributed to the press, and the next day newspapers across the country printed it in its entirety. It stated, "I do order and declare that all persons held as slaves within said designated States, and parts of States, are, and henceforward shall be free." The "designated" areas were those that were still in rebellion and had seceded from the Union. The second paragraph asked freed slaves "to abstain from all violence," advising that they "labor faithfully for reasonable wages." Moreover, they "will be received into the armed service of the United States."

In reality, at the time it was issued, the Emancipation Proclamation had no real authority, because Lincoln had no authority over the Southern states to which it was directed.

Black troops in the Civil War

With Lincoln's January 1, 1863, Emancipation Proclamation and executive order, and the subsequent call for black troops, Union war aims and black goals converged. Once blacks could simultaneously fight for the Union and slaves, black leaders across the North hailed the change as the opportunity they had been seeking—a patriotic and courageous call to arms that would validate decades of anti-slavery efforts.

Black military service, they believed, would help dismantle the institution of slavery and undermine claims of racial inferiority, the first step in ending prejudice and establishing claims to equal citizenship in the postwar nation. Participation in the war became an abolitionist act, an opportunity to obtain "indemnity for the past, and security for the future." More than 186,000 blacks served in the Union Army and 18,000 served in the Union Navy.

Despite their willingness to serve, black troops suffered unendurable discrimination. The poor treatment of black soldiers was a reflection of widespread racist attitudes. Once enlisted, blacks were first considered laborers instead of soldiers. Black soldiers were assigned to menial back-breaking tasks, such as ditch digging and collecting dead bodies. Their equipment, clothes, guns, and food were inferior, as was the case with their medical care and compensation. Many of the black soldiers protested this unfair treatment. Sergeant William Walker, of the Third South Carolina Volunteers, led his company in a protest against the inequities in the Union Army. Walker was court-martialed and executed. Others protesting the unequal treatment were either shot or locked in jail.

Victory in the end

The Emancipation Proclamation was, as Lincoln admitted, a military necessity, not a humanitarian measure; it was a strike against the Confederacy, not on behalf of the slave. It was an unavoidable war measure and "is per se," the *Weekly Anglo-African* announced, "no more humanitarian than a hundred pounder rifled cannon."

The proclamation came two years after the start of the war, freed only some slaves, and exempted slaves in the border states or those owned by "loyal" masters, thus reinforcing slavery in parts of the South. The legal end to slavery everywhere in the United States did not come until the enactment of the Thirteenth Amendment in 1865. Well-attuned to the half-hearted efforts of professed friends, blacks saw that Lincoln had done the least, rather than the most, against slavery.

Nonetheless, the North's victory in the Civil War essentially secured the abolition of slavery in America. The black leaders of the nineteenth century were persistent and unrelenting in their efforts to insure that slavery and racial injustice remained a single, focused issue in their time. As a result, they helped to move America toward a more tolerant society.

Blacks standing together during slavery and the abolition movement

Blacks demonstrated leadership in many ways during our nineteenth-century Historical Challenge. Throughout the era, black people stood together as families, churches, societies, and communities, always persevering in spite of unspeakable abuse and odds. Slaves and free blacks worked as businesspeople, earning money to buy freedom for themselves and loved ones. We fought for America's independence in the Revolutionary War, in spite of racial discrimination and broken promises of freedom. We asserted our right to be in America, and refused to be sent to Liberia.

In the North in particular, we bought businesses and real estate, and sent our children to the same schools as whites. We wrote books, articles, pamphlets, and speeches. We spoke out in churches and public venues. We formed societies dedicated to abolition. Some of our people were members of the older black elite class of educated and wealthy businessmen. Others were younger and came to leadership by way of slavery.

We filed lawsuits, persevered through appeals, and challenged High Court decisions.

Our people supported John Brown and the raid on Harpers Ferry. We fought in the Civil War, as we had in the Revolutionary War, despite rampant discrimination.

Ultimately, we persevered to help gain the passage of the Thirteenth Amendment outlawing slavery in 1865.

No other group's suffering can surpass ours. Furthermore, African-Americans' contributions to the making of America are without equal. America as we know it today would not exist without the struggle and contributions of African-Americans.

"We shall not forget you."

Black abolitionists left a permanent mark on America's heritage, culture, and institutions. Their generous contributions to the nation's understanding of the meaning of freedom and justice are immeasurable. Continuing to tell the stories of the conviction, struggle, and sacrifices of black and white abolitionists is paramount to ensuring that African-Americans never forget their contributions to statehood, life, liberty, and the pursuit of happiness.

Let us adopt the "we shall not forget you" attitude of the mostly free black population of the North, who kept fueling the fire of the abolition movement and would not allow it to burn out. They truly played a major role in advancing the resistance movement of African-Americans and transforming America.

The abolition movement broke the chains and tore down the walls of institutionalized slavery. Unfortunately, the resistance of white society to this freedom gave rise to the Historical Challenge that African-Americans would face in the twentieth century—the one-hundred-year struggle for civil rights.

Our Twentieth-Century Historical Challenge: The Civil Rights Movement

A long-awaited ray of hope

Lincoln's December 1863 "Proclamation of Amnesty and Reconstruction" was intended to start bringing the South back into the Union. On April 9, 1865, the trampled and weary Confederacy, under the leadership of President Jefferson Davis, surrendered, thereby ending the Civil War.

The third quarter of the 1800s was a triumphant period for blacks, with the passage of the Thirteenth, Fourteenth, and Fifteenth Amendments to the Constitution. These amendments abolished slavery and gave blacks citizenship, equal access to public facilities, and the right to vote—providing a long-awaited ray of hope in a dark period of their history in America.

The Reconstruction Act of 1867, passed by Congress, which overrode the veto of President Andrew Johnson, called for a new constitution in each state. Freed male slaves were able to vote, and they used their votes to replace many Confederates in public office.

In his book *From Jim Crow to Civil Rights*, Michael J. Klarman states:

> Reconstruction was, in fact, the basic issue of the Civil War. The desire to remake the South, to reorganize its social system, to bring its divergent economy into the mainstream of American life, to impose peculiar concepts of government and of constitutional interpretation upon the Southern states had been the reason for beginning the war and for prosecuting it with vigor, despite tremendous losses in human life and costs in national wealth.

But freedom and the right to vote were meaningless without financial and social equality and opportunity. There were great black leaders who understood this early on, and they spoke publicly about it.

Black leaders speak out

Frederick Douglass saw the dangers of an African-American population permanently relegated to poverty. In 1886, Douglass told a crowd in Washington, D.C.:

> Where justice is denied, where poverty is enforced, where ignorance prevails, and where any one class is made to feel that society is in an organized conspiracy to oppress, rob, and degrade them, neither persons nor property will be safe.

Douglass and other leaders were largely ignored. Whites conspired to limit black participation in voting, education, and economic opportunities.

During this period, blacks led the push for creating free public education for both black and white children in the South. Blacks were further encouraged by the enactment of the Civil Rights Act of 1875, which made it unlawful to discriminate in public facilities. However, for all the good that resulted from Reconstruction, there were still barriers.

Reconstruction gains quickly lost

The Freemen's Bureau was a post-Civil War federal agency whose primary responsibility, ostensibly, was to ease the transition of former slaves into mainstream society. However, its staff apparently also consisted of a number of whites with racist views. Some of its restrictive policies presented terrible setbacks for the former slave's progress in gaining economic, social, and political independence.

For example, the Bureau introduced a policy of forced labor with a regulation stating that if a black man refused to sign a contract and accept a job, he would be forced to work for no pay. White employers immediately seized the opportunity to use this regulation to abuse blacks just emancipated from slavery.

Most of the rights that blacks gained during Reconstruction were quickly lost following the 1876 election of President

Rutherford B. Hayes. While campaigning for office, Hayes had promised that he would withdraw all federal troops from the South if elected. As promised, federal troops left the South in April 1877, effectively ending the Reconstruction Era and abandoning African-Americans in the South, leaving them at the mercy of white-controlled local and state governments.

President Hayes' decision, in effect, rolled back all the gains that blacks made during and after the Civil War. It was the beginning of the "Jim Crow" era and the new twentieth-century Historical Challenge for African-Americans.

Who was Jim Crow?

Jim Crow was not a person, but a term that some believe came about from a white minstrel show act performed by a man named Thomas "Daddy" Rice, who blackened his face, danced a demeaning jig, and sang a song with lyrics that included the words, "Jump Jim Crow." Jim Crow was believed to be a slave owner. The song was insulting and spread a vicious message of black inferiority.

The spread of Jim Crow laws

In 1881, the State of Tennessee passed a law requiring railroad companies to furnish separate cars for black passengers. This act would lead to other Southern states initiating similar laws.

Armed with the security that the federal government would no longer interfere, Jim Crow laws that codified segregation and other forms of racial discrimination were passed all over the South.

Under the banner of "state rights," these laws included:

• Voter discrimination practices such as grandfather clauses (laws that restricted the right to vote to people whose ancestors had voted before the Civil War)

• Poll taxes (fees charged to poor blacks)

• Literacy tests (such as naming all the Supreme Court justices throughout America's history, though illiterate whites were allowed to vote)

• Property requirements and intimidation at the polls with "white only" primaries

In addition, the education system had become separate and unequal, if it was available at all.

The High Court supports Jim Crow

U.S. Supreme Court rulings backed these Jim Crow laws, undermining the intents of the new constitutional amendments that ostensibly had secured civil rights for black citizens.

In 1873, the High Court ruled that the Fourteenth Amendment only covered those rights received under federal citizenship, and the right to vote was still a right of the state.

On the centennial anniversary of America's Independence in 1876, the High Court ruled that the Fifteenth Amendment did not guarantee national citizens the right to vote, giving Southern states further ammunition to disenfranchise black voters.

In 1883, the Supreme Court ruled that the public accommodation portion of the Civil Rights Act of 1875, which prohibited discrimination in public facilities, was unconstitutional, thus giving states the right to create segregated facilities.

And then there was its landmark 1896 decision in *Plessy v. Ferguson*, where the High Court ruled 7-1 that "separate but equal" public facilities for blacks and whites were legal.

When Mississippi amended its constitution to eliminate voting rights for blacks in 1890, other states in the South quickly followed suit. Without the right to vote, blacks were powerless to change segregation laws. The same laws also prevented some poor whites from voting. And no woman of any color had the right to vote at that time.

The U.S. Supreme Court, in its deliberate efforts to erode the legal protections and freedom of African-Americans under the new amendments, had effectively given these new state and local Jim Crow laws its stamp of approval.

The white South had risen once again, and segregation was the law of the land.

Black leaders stand up for justice

The black leadership of this time did not passively accept these setbacks. They used every forum possible, from church pulpits to the press to courtrooms, to appeal for justice.

Blacks first attacked the courts with a flood of civil rights cases. During this time, there was a major migration of blacks from the South to the North and West—but their efforts did not quell the rising tide of vicious and violent efforts of whites to strip them of the hard-fought rights they had won.

Whites in the South began to form organizations like the Ku Klux Klan, White Citizen Council, and the White Brotherhood, as an attempt to strike fear into the hearts and minds of blacks and to control the black populations in the South. They systematically inflicted lynchings, castrations, beatings, and shootings of blacks as a way of exercising and maintaining control. Barely twenty years after dismantling Reconstruction, white Southerners achieved a complete reversal of all the gains blacks had made.

Differing viewpoints

There was not a consensus by the black leadership on ways to approach the civil rights challenge. Booker T. Washington did not believe that the fight for civil rights should be the primary focus of blacks. His philosophy was for blacks to give up the fight for social, political, and constitutional rights, for the sake of gaining economic opportunity. In his famous "Atlanta Compromise" speech of 1895, Washington said, "The wisest among my race understand that the agitation of questions of social equality is the extremist folly [. . .]."

Washington, founder and president of Tuskegee Institute in Alabama, was considered the most powerful black leader of his time. He believed that blacks should focus on developing skills, buying property, and achieving economic power. His message attracted thousands of followers and won him friends in high places. He dined with President Theodore Roosevelt and served as a consultant to the president on federal appointments.

In Washington's view, blacks were not ready for true citizenship; what most blacks considered rights, he saw as privileges. But other black leaders were convinced that the issues at hand were civil rights and citizenship, and there could be no substitute.

The U.S. Supreme Court's Plessy decision, which in effect denied African-Americans their newly won constitutional rights, set the stage for the intense drama called the Civil Rights Movement. Coming on the heels of the abolition movement, this battle for black civil rights carried over into the twentieth century, with new leaders.

Racism and segregation persist

At the turn of the century, many African-Americans found themselves living in conditions not very different from those they experienced before the Civil War. Many in the South were still tied to the land as sharecroppers, a farming system where they rented land and equipment from a white landowner. They received food on credit until harvest time, when they sold their crops and paid off the landowner and other creditors. But with the contract tilted much to the landowner's favor, black farmers barely had enough money left to provide for their families.

Blacks had already lost the right to vote, as well as other civil rights that they had once enjoyed during Reconstruction. Institutionalized racism and perpetuated segregation prevailed. Laws and courts turned blind eyes to violence against blacks carried out by the Ku Klux Klan and other anti-black groups, in many cases on behalf of local governments. For instance, over 3,700 lynchings occurred in the early part of the twentieth century, inspiring race riots that led to backlashes from the white community.

These horrible conditions inspired a new generation of black leadership to fight back and form more organized civil rights efforts.

An increasing number of blacks pursued higher education, and a larger black bourgeoisie class emerged. These new leaders were guided by a desire to change the conditions of their people, whose lives were under constant threat. They could no longer solely rely on the North, who had supported their cause prior to the Civil War, nor the courts. But they would press on, using every available weapon to ensure that the civil rights they once possessed would eventually be theirs again.

To fill the void left by the great black abolitionist Frederick Douglass, many leaders would come forward—leaders such as William Monroe Trottler, who founded the *Guardian* newspaper in Boston in 1901. Trottler's paper was instrumental in waging the war on Booker T. Washington's accommodationist approach to the African-American struggle.

Another black leader emerged at this time. His name was W.E.B. Du Bois, and he is considered by many to be the father of the Civil Rights Movement.

W.E.B. Du Bois

Du Bois was born in 1868 in Massachusetts. He first attended all-black Fisk University in Nashville, Tennessee, before going on to Harvard University, where he became the first black to receive a PhD. He was a constant critic of Booker T. Washington's views, insisting that blacks not concede their political and civil rights. He was convinced that blacks must insist on legal equality as a basic right and as a fundamental component of improving their condition.

In 1905, Du Bois, along with several other black leaders such as J. Max Barber, Alonzo Herndon, and Frederick McGhee, formed the Niagara Movement. It called for universal manhood suffrage, economic opportunities, and civil rights for blacks. Du Bois, speaking on the goals of the Niagara Movement, said, "We want full manhood suffrage and we want it now [. . .]. We want discrimination in public accommodation to cease [. . .]. We want the Constitution of the country enforced [. . .]. We are men! We will be treated as men. And we shall win!"

The founding of the NAACP

When the Niagara Movement fell on hard times, Du Bois joined with several white reformists to found the National Association for the Advancement of Colored People (NAACP) in 1909. Oswald Garrison Villard, the grandson of abolitionist William Lloyd Garrison, was one of the founding members.

The NAACP was an outgrowth of a meeting called by the National Negro Conference to discuss issues pertaining to racial justice—in particular, the race riot that had taken place in Springfield, Illinois, in 1908, claiming the lives of eight blacks. The NAACP had as its objective to "secure for all people the rights guaranteed in the Thirteenth, Fourteenth, and Fifteenth amendments to the U.S. Constitution." These amendments, delivered during the Civil War era, had declared an end to slavery, equal protection under the law, and universal suffrage.

Many considered W.E.B. Du Bois the intellectual force in the NAACP's early years, and he served as the founder and editor of its journal, *The Crisis*. Those holding executive leadership positions in the organization read like a *Who's Who* of blacks in the Civil Rights Movement, including James Weldon Johnson, Walter White, and Roy Wilkins. Thurgood Marshall, who would later become the first black member of the U.S. Supreme Court, and Charles Houston led the NAACP's legal defense fund.

Initially the organization operated primarily in the North, though close to ninety percent of all American blacks lived in the South. The organization, which had an all-white board with the exception of Du Bois, grew very slowly. However, this changed with the first wave of blacks moving from the South to the North, and with the NAACP's victories in the courts. By the time of Booker T. Washington's death in 1915, this new twentieth-century movement—the Civil Rights Movement—was solidly in the hands of black leaders like W.E.B. Du Bois and Marcus Garvey.

Other approaches to justice for African-Americans

Marcus Garvey was born in Jamaica in 1887 and moved to Harlem, New York, in 1916, where he founded the Universal Negro Improvement Association (UNIA). Considered a "black nationalist," Garvey developed the UNIA into one of the wealthiest and largest black organizations in America. In 1919, he formed the Black Star Line, his steamship company that was dedicated to transporting African-Americans to Africa. He also created the Negro Factories Corporation to support black-owned factories across the U.S. and the Caribbean.

"For the Negro to depend on the ballot and his industrial progress alone will be hopeless," Garvey said, "as it does not help him when he is lynched, burned, Jim-Crowed and segregated. The future of the Negro therefore, outside of Africa, spells ruin and disaster." Garvey advocated a single solution to the problems of blacks in America: emigration to Africa.

During the Great Migration of the 1920s, African-Americans migrated in droves to the North, but didn't find the political, social, and economic opportunities that they were searching for. Blacks remained the last hired and first fired, disproportionately relegated to low-skilled and poorly paying jobs. Residential segregation prevailed, confining blacks to poor neighborhoods. Black schools did not provide the same level of education for African-American migrants, and so they had less of a chance to move up the economic and social ladder than their white counterparts. When African-Americans pushed the limits of this informal system of apartheid, seeking housing in predominantly white neighborhoods, they were physically turned out.

Challenging "separate but equal"

The NAACP's record, including public campaigns against lynching and fighting for blacks' civil rights in the courts, placed it on the forefront of the black struggle during the first fifty years of the twentieth century.

In the 1930s, the NAACP reached a defining moment. It was the worst of times for Americans in general, and African-Americans in particular. The stock market had crashed in 1929. The rate of unemployment was fifty percent for blacks in the big cities, coupled with a Congress and a President that refused to institute racial reform or address the realities of the Great Depression. Unable to bring about change through legislation, the NAACP took the fight to the courts.

A plan of approach was developed by Harvard-educated NAACP lawyer Nathan Ross Marigold. *The Marigold Report*, as it became known, was written in 1933, and showed that the Southern states had not met the test of the Fourteenth Amendment, which called for establishing "separate but equal" facilities. Marigold called for the NAACP to challenge the concept of "separate but equal" by claiming that it violated the equal protection clause of the amendment.

Charles H. Houston and Thurgood Marshall started the ball rolling in the courts, bringing about real change through legal action. Case after case challenged the concept of separate but equal in transportation, educational opportunities, and white election primaries. Throughout the 1940s and 1950s, Marshall and a team of NAACP constitutional lawyers won a series of precedent-setting cases that led to the landmark *Brown vs. Board of Education* decision in 1954.

A historic victory

In *Brown v. Board of Education of Topeka, Kansas,* the U.S. Supreme Court unanimously agreed that segregation in public schools was unconstitutional. This decision set the groundwork for widespread desegregation.

In this case, the NAACP's lawyers did not merely point out differences in per-student expenditures; they also brought in social scientists who demonstrated that education must be measured by the total environment and psychological impact of the education on children. This included the famous doll tests conducted by black psychologists Kenneth and Mamie Clark, who studied the impact of segregation on the self-esteem of black children. Kenneth Clark argued, "Segregation was, is, the way in which a society tells a group of human beings they are inferior to other groups of human beings in the society. Children internalize this view. As a result, separate could never be equal."

White resistance to desegregation

The landmark court ruling was extremely difficult to enforce. State and local governments did everything they could to fight desegregation in the schools, leading up to the Little Rock Central High School standoff in 1957, when nine black students were ordered barred from the school by Governor Orval Faubus, causing President Eisenhower to send in federal troops to protect the students.

The NAACP continued to fight to overturn Jim Crow laws everywhere they existed, inspiring its members to stand up to segregation. In 1955, Rosa Parks refused to give up her seat on a bus to a white passenger, motivating blacks around the country to take personal action.

The nonviolent movement meets violent opposition

After Rosa Parks' act of bravery, Dr. Martin Luther King, Jr., the newly elected president of the Montgomery Improvement Association, led a bus boycott for over a year. In 1957, Dr. King became the president of the Southern Christian Leadership Conference (SCLC). The SCLC developed into a major force in leading a nonviolent Civil Rights Movement, using civil disobedience as its weapon.

Black students, as a part of SNCC (Student Nonviolent Coordinating Committee), held sit-ins across the South, in schools, libraries, theaters, restaurants, and swimming pools—wherever they were denied service or entrance. SNCC members also had a major role in voter registration across the South, in particular Georgia, Mississippi, and Alabama.

In 1961, the Congress of Racial Equality (CORE) launched the Freedom Riders program, sending black and white volunteers on buses throughout the South to challenge segregated interstate travel laws and facilities. Early in their efforts, a mob in Alabama torched one of the Freedom Riders' buses. This kind of violence only strengthened the resolve of the Civil Rights Movement activists.

In 1963, Mississippi NAACP Field Secretary Medgar Evers was assassinated in my home state of Mississippi. Dr. Martin Luther King, Jr., was jailed in Birmingham and called on all individuals to disobey unjust laws. Later that year, Dr. King delivered the famous "I Have a Dream" speech to over 250,000 people from the steps of the Lincoln Memorial during the March on Washington.

1964: A watershed year for civil rights

The Twenty-Fourth Amendment was passed in 1964. It outlawed the poll tax, which prevented blacks and poor whites from voting in the South.

Following lobbying, protest, and mass demonstrations in the South, Congress passed, and President Johnson signed, the Civil

Rights Act of 1964. The Act prohibited any discrimination based on race, color, religion, or national origin. This gave the federal government the power to enforce desegregation. Section 201 (a) of the Act states:

> All persons shall be entitled to the full and equal enjoyment of the goods, services, facilities, privileges, advantages, and accommodations of any place of public accommodation, as defined in this section, without discrimination or segregation on the ground of race, color, religion, or national origin.

1965: Selma

The Selma, Alabama, voter registration campaign was first organized in 1963 by African-American citizens, the Dallas County (Alabama) Voters League, and the SNCC. The campaign continued into 1964, but the people had to deal with violent attacks and constant legal and economic opposition from white county officials and citizens.

In July 1964, President Johnson signed the Civil Rights Act, prohibiting segregation of public facilities. Nevertheless, Jim Crow persisted in Selma and other places throughout the South. Later in 1964, to keep the voter registration campaign going, the Dallas County Voters League asked for help from the SCLC, and they accepted the call. In response, white politicians stepped up their oppressive tactics, and law enforcement escalated their violence against registrants and marchers.

In January 1965, the Selma Voting Rights Campaign officially started, with Dr. Martin Luther King, Jr., speaking on behalf of the movement. Dr. King and President Johnson agreed at that time to move forward on voting rights legislation. In February 1965, Malcolm X advocated for the Selma Voting Rights Campaign; President Johnson spoke out in support of it; and Dr. King, SCLC staff, and members of Congress met in Selma for strategy sessions. Marches and other forms of nonviolent civil disobedience took place in nearby counties.

Jimmie Lee Jackson killed by law enforcement

James Orange, a field worker with the SCLC, was arrested during a nonviolent protest in nearby Perry County. To protest his arrest, on the night of February 18, 1965, approximately five hundred people left Zion United Methodist Church in Marion, Alabama, and attempted a peaceful walk to the Perry County Jail about a half a block away, where Mr. Orange was being held. A line of Marion City police, sheriff's deputies, and Alabama state troopers ambushed them. Streetlights were abruptly turned off and the police began to beat the protesters.

Twenty-six-year-old Jimmie Lee Jackson ran with his mother and grandfather into Mack's Café behind the church. They were pursued by Alabama state troopers, and the troopers began to attack them in the restaurant. As Mr. Jackson tried to protect his mother, Alabama state trooper James Fowler shot him twice in the abdomen. Mr. Jackson died at Good Samaritan Hospital in Selma eight days later.

The first march: Bloody Sunday

Jimmie Lee Jackson's death prompted the call to march from Selma to Montgomery for the right to vote. The march took place on Sunday, March 7, 1965. On that fateful day, six hundred people, marching peacefully two by two, headed east out of Selma on U.S. Route 80. They got only as far as the Edmund Pettus Bridge six blocks away, where state and local lawmen on horseback attacked them with billy clubs and tear gas. Seventeen marchers were hospitalized, and many others were beaten and brutalized. That day became known as Bloody Sunday.

Immediately after the brutal attacks on the peaceful marchers, Dr. King sent a telegram around the country. He asked for ministers of all faiths to travel to Selma and march to Montgomery on Tuesday, March 9, two days after Bloody Sunday. The Federal District Court simultaneously issued a restraining order prohibiting the march. With two thousand to three thousand people of all races waiting to march, Dr. King made a decision to continue the march in defiance of the Federal District Court order.

The second march: Turnaround Tuesday

The second march began on March 9, 1965. The marchers sang "Ain't Gonna Let Nobody Turn Me Round." The Alabama state troopers met them when they once again reached the bottom of the Edmund Pettus Bridge. The marchers dropped to their knees and prayed. After the prayer, they rose, turned, and marched back to Brown Chapel Church, avoiding another confrontation with state troopers and skirting the issue of whether to obey the Federal District Court's order. This march became known as Turnaround Tuesday.

The third march: Selma to Montgomery

Finally, the Federal District Court granted permission for the Selma to Montgomery march. On Sunday, March 21, 1965, over 3,500 people of all races, including ministers of all faiths, leaders from major civil rights organizations, and celebrities, marched together in support of voting rights for African-Americans.

Bloody Sunday, Turnaround Tuesday, and the Selma to Montgomery march all helped lead to the August passage of the Voting Rights Act of 1965.

August 1965: Congress passes the Voting Rights Act

The Voting Rights Act, extended in 1970, 1975, and 1982, is without a doubt one of the single most important pieces of civil rights legislation ever adopted by the United States Congress.

> The Act makes good on the Fifteenth Amendment by permanently guaranteeing that no person shall be denied the right to vote on account of race or color.

> Section 4 of the Act ended the use of literacy requirements for voting in six Southern states (Alabama, Georgia, Louisiana, Mississippi, South Carolina, and Virginia) and in many counties of North Carolina.

> Under Section 5 of the Act, no voting law changes were legally enforceable in these jurisdictions until approved either by a three-judge court in the District of Columbia or by the Attorney General of the United States.

The heart of the Voting Rights Act struck down in 2013

In June 2013, the U.S. Supreme Court "effectively struck down the heart of the Voting Rights Act of 1965," as the *New York Times* reported. The High Court ruled 5-4 that nine states could circumvent Section 5 and change their election laws without the required notice and federal approval. The nine states requesting this permission are mostly in the South, but the Supreme Court's ruling sets dangerous precedent for all fifty states.

In a vehement dissent to the ruling, Justice Ruth Bader Ginsburg wrote:

> Beyond question, the Voting Rights Act is no ordinary legislation. It is extraordinary because Congress embarked on a mission long delayed and of extraordinary importance: to realize the purpose and promise of the Fifteenth Amendment [. . .].
>
> For a half century, a concerted effort has been made to end racial discrimination in voting. Thanks to the Voting Rights Act, progress once the subject of a dream has been achieved and continues to be made [. . .].
>
> The court errs egregiously by overriding Congress's decision.

Moving forward, meeting violence, making history

A wave of legal change, violence, and protests moved the fight for civil rights forward. Civil rights workers, black and white, were killed in riots, through police brutality during peaceful marches, and at the hands of the Ku Klux Klan during efforts to sign up black voters. Race riots erupted in Los Angeles, Detroit, and Newark, New Jersey. Malcolm X was assassinated in 1965 at the age of thirty-nine. Just three years later, in 1968, Martin Luther King, Jr., was assassinated, also at the age of thirty-nine.

President Johnson issued an executive order for affirmative action, and laws prohibiting interracial marriage were overturned. Johnson then signed the new Civil Rights Act of 1968, prohibiting discrimination in the sale, rental, or refinancing of housing. This action all but ended the battle for civil rights as a dominant challenge for African-Americans of the twentieth century.

Black leadership during Jim Crow and the Civil Rights Movement

African-Americans demonstrated leadership in many ways during our twentieth-century Historical Challenge. Just as we had done throughout the nineteenth-century challenge, black people stood together as families, churches, societies, and communities in the face of rampant discrimination and abuse.

African-American men voted and used those votes to unseat many Confederates in public office. We filed lawsuits and spoke out in churches, the press, courtrooms, and other public venues to defend our rights to free public education, economic opportunities, and access to public facilities.

We pursued higher education, entered professional fields, and created an expanded black bourgeoisie class. We founded newspapers, colleges, and organizations like the NAACP. The NAACP led public campaigns and took strong legal action in defense of our civil rights.

We took courageous steps in nonviolent acts of civil disobedience. We went to jail for the cause. We died in riots, lynchings, and assassinations.

Our people lobbied, protested, held mass demonstrations, and persevered until the passage of the Civil Rights Acts of 1964 and the Voting Rights Acts of 1965.

Moving into the Economic Empowerment (Silver Rights) era

There is no question that the Civil Rights Movement accomplished its objective: securing for African-Americans their constitutional rights that had been promised but denied for one hundred years.

However, this significant movement was never intended as a remedy to counteract the barriers and disparities that had effectively hampered black economic progress in our four-hundred-year history in America. It did put us in a position to pursue and acquire wealth. Now the time has come for us to build this economic power in the African-American community.

Our Twenty-First-Century Historical Challenge: Converting Political Power to Economic Power

The Civil Rights Movement elevated blacks' status from that of second-class citizens to one of many opportunities—most importantly, the opportunity to convert our political power to economic power. Now we must seize these opportunities by refocusing our energy, time, and resources toward the Historical Challenge of achieving economic power in the twenty-first century.

The urgency of now

We have accomplished a great deal over the last fifty years in terms of education and professional and political achievements. But we can ill afford to be complacent about our current economic position. The global shifts currently taking place could threaten our future prosperity if we are not careful to act in a manner that will protect our future. This economic power that I speak of has a sense of urgency about it, because the world around us is undergoing profound changes right before our eyes, and the stakes are incredibly high.

Twenty years ago, who would have believed that we would be speaking of China as a world leader in manufacturing output? And I don't mean cheap goods, but value-added products. What about India, today's world leader in call center support and software outsourcing?

And what about the Internet and information technology? It wasn't long ago that the Internet was merely a test case. Now it has produced or enhanced the rise of near-instant communication by electronic mail, instant messaging, Voice over Internet Protocol (VoIP) telephone calls, two-way interactive video calls, and the World Wide Web with its discussion forums, blogs, social networking, and e-commerce. Those who are able to take advantage of the Internet's power will find themselves at the forefront of acquiring some of the greatest margins of wealth in the history of the world.

I'm talking life-changing forces here. This progress is dramatically raising the standards of living in China and India; they have now joined the new global economy. African-Americans must do the same.

Four driving forces

I believe that there are four forces driving this new global economy:

- Innovation

- Information

- Distribution networks that deliver this information

- The sources of capital that finance each of these

Those who control these forces are seeing tremendous economic growth and gains in productivity. Our world in the decades ahead is a world of great potential for advances in the acquisition of wealth. It will also be a world of intense competition, not just for African-Americans, but for all people.

A good social agenda is just an empty promise without a sound economic agenda.

As I travel around the nation, I hear both anxiety and anticipation. I can see it in any number of discussions—from strengthening health care, to improving education, to curing AIDS, caring for the elderly, poverty, childcare, black on black crime, and police brutality, just to name a few.

These are all important and noteworthy issues that threaten the very fabric of African-American communities. But the solution to all of these issues is inescapably tied to our ability to acquire economic power. A good social agenda is just an empty promise without a sound economic agenda. This is the reality of the twenty-first century and our Historical Challenge.

A sustainable and diverse economy

I want to focus on the importance of African-Americans developing a new agenda that will enhance our ability to sustain a high standard of living, with good jobs and healthy communities.

There will be serious social and economic consequences for African-Americans, for present and future generations, if we do not make Economic Empowerment our top priority.

If our communities are going to grow and become stable entities, they must possess a sustainable and diverse economy that empowers businesses, community members, and the many other components that interact within the community. This economic power:

- Creates jobs
- Provides reinvestment capital and income-earning opportunities
- Supports business growth and expansion
- Reduces crime and poverty
- Contributes to the quality of life
- Ultimately provides stability for the community

Economic Empowerment is a process, not an event.

Accomplishing all this will require that we view Economic Empowerment as a shared issue that is fulfilled by a process, not an event. Acquiring wealth by such means as winning the lottery or inheriting riches is an event; but real and sustainable economic power happens over a period of time as a result of a strategic process. And the process requires that we understand the components of what I call the Circle of Wealth, and adopt it as a historic strategy.

The Circle of Wealth

If the twenty-first-century challenge for African-Americans is economic power, and I believe it is, then the key components in the Circle of Wealth must find strategic ways to achieve it.

My definition for the Circle of Wealth is a derivative of the old African proverb, "It takes a whole village to raise a child." To grow an economy takes many different components of the African-American "village" or community—the collective components that we control or influence.

These components or roles can forge a collective effort sufficient to build the new economy that's necessary for Economic Empowerment in the Silver Rights era. Successfully harnessing and directing our collective *political* power will ultimately lead to collective *economic* power, as we reverse the rapid decay in our communities and achieve an unrivaled advantage in the world economy. However, if we fail, we will pay a heavy price in lost opportunities, and we will face an uphill battle in growing our economy and acquiring wealth.

The Circle of Wealth principle encompasses seven core components. These components form the foundation for driving the process of Economic Empowerment in the African-American community.

The components are:

1. Messengers

2. Agitators

3. Supporters

4. Primers

5. Partners

6. Leaders

7. Drivers

MESSENGERS: Using the power of information and communication

Messengers craft the message of Economic Empowerment so that it can be communicated and transmitted to the people. Messengers will help African-Americans understand that Economic Empowerment is our twenty-first-century Historical Challenge, and explain why a movement to address it is vital to our future.

Messengers include:

- The black media

- Black journalists working in mainstream media

- Black political leadership, national and local

- Religious leaders

- Artists, songwriters, musicians, poets, writers, and bloggers

- Professional athletes, actors, and actresses

- Others with the power to influence our culture at the local and national levels

Let me pause here to speak to Artists about the role Artists played as Messengers in the twentieth-century Historical Challenge.

The music of Artist-Messengers like Sam Cooke, James Brown, Curtis Mayfield, Harold Melvin and The Blue Notes, and Marvin Gaye interpreted the conditions of the people, inspired them to take on the challenge, and motivated them to achieve the Historical Challenge of their time.

The Artist-Messenger Sam Cooke made his timeless recording of "A Change Is Gonna Come" in 1963. The song is about the struggle of African-Americans and contains the refrain, "It's been a long time coming, but I know a change is gonna come." It is said that the song was inspired by personal events in Cooke's life, most prominently an event in which he and his entourage were turned away from a whites-only motel in Shreveport, Louisiana. The song was written to speak to Cooke's struggle and the struggle of African-Americans at the time.

"A Change Is Gonna Come" became an anthem for the Civil Rights Movement.

The Artist-Messenger group known as The Impressions featuring Curtis Mayfield recorded their hit, "We're a Winner," which was an uplifting composition whose lyrics encouraged African-Americans that the time for self-pity is over, and that one should acknowledge his or her worth, even in the face of opposition.

"Say It Loud – I'm Black and I'm Proud" is a song by the Artist-Messenger James Brown. The song was released in 1968 and held the #1 spot on the R&B singles chart for six weeks. The song became an unofficial anthem of the African-American struggle at the time.

Now contrast those empowering and timeless messages of pride and unity with a great deal of today's music, which, although creative, is degrading. It makes a mockery of our women and creates a false sense of reality for our children, keeping them in a state of suspended animation as they sing destructive songs all day long—all while the world leaves them behind. There's a lot of sex but no love.

The Artists of today, principally so-called gangster rappers, use their God-given talent to make music that degrades. They hijack the minds and energy of our young people and redirect them toward counterproductive thinking and actions.

Instead, the Artists of today must embrace their challenge to be Artist-Messengers who deliver the message of Economic Empowerment to African-Americans—following the example of the Artist-Messengers who have gone on before them.

While we are discussing children, I want to challenge the old assertion that "the children are our future."

The children are not our future; we are their future—and if we fail to pursue the Historical Challenge before us, they will not have a future.

Not all rappers are falling prey to an industry that is DEAD set on promoting and pushing toxic messages to our young folk, all in the name of making money. So I would be incorrect if I didn't give artists like my friend David Banner respect.

Rapper David Banner

David Banner, a Mississippian, is using his voice to awaken a generation of young people to the challenge of today with songs like "Evil Knievil," with lyrics like:

> They gave us Obama like
> It was gonna stop the fight
> Like it was gonna stop the cause
> Folks still scraping
> Trying to find them some socks and drawers
> And something to eat
> The IRS is coming so I'm back on these beats…
> I was on my way to heaven but I stopped and turned around for my people
> I'll try to never leave you
> This is a war against evil [. . .]

We must find ways to use the power of this very persuasive artistic talent to carry the message of Economic Empowerment to our young people, and help shape it as the highest priority for African-Americans in the twenty-first century.

AGITATORS: Advocating for African-Americans' advancement

Agitators are African-American organizations that have been established on the premise of advancing the social, political, and economic conditions of African-Americans. As part of their mission, they work against forces and conditions that hinder our progress.

Agitators include:

- Fraternities
- Sororities
- Social and professional organizations
- Black business associations
- Political organizations

These leaders are on the forefront of the Economic Empowerment movement by:

- Fighting for greater procurement opportunities for black-owned businesses in the public sector

- Lobbying elected officials for laws and other legal remedies that will aid black businesses

- Motivating Corporate America to do business with black-owned businesses to grow and support them, thus investing in the African-American community's economic stability and the stability of the overall U.S. economy

SUPPORTERS: Individual consumers with collective buying power

Supporters are the consumers in the Circle of Wealth.

They are us: the African-Americans with a collective annual buying power of more than $1 trillion.

That kind of buying power can help amass great wealth for those whose products and services these Supporters consume. Supporters who spend their money with black businesses help expand those businesses, thus creating more jobs and enriching their own communities.

Those of us who understand the principle of the Circle of Wealth must help all Supporters understand the true value of the dollar, and how it represents a critical link in the Circle of Wealth and all our futures. This understanding is crucial to the success of the Economic Empowerment movement.

Supporters have the power to change the financial conditions of the African-American community—and we must encourage each other to use this power.

PRIMERS/ECONOMIC ENGINES: Entities and institutions with massive budgets to spend

Primers are public and private entities that African-Americans directly control, including:

- Public school boards
- Colleges and universities
- Supervisors and commissioners

- Mayors' offices

- City councils

- The procurement offices that buy products and services for these entities, institutions, and elected bodies

With a few exceptions, African-American individuals in this group have ascended to their positions of power and influence as a result of opportunities created by the successes of the Civil Rights Movement. Most of these individuals serve in predominantly black cities and districts, elected by the voting power of blacks.

In return, they should feel obligated to use the power they exercise to transform the communities and lives of the people who granted them the privilege to serve.

These Primers usually control massive budgets. Their objective should be to find legal ways to redirect some of the dollars in their budgets toward the black business owners, or Drivers, in their communities. Ultimately, it is the Drivers whose investment dollars will begin to solve the problems of poverty, crime, and other social ills in their cities.

Primers should not be viewed as the sole source of procurement opportunities for the black business class. Rather, Primers create the environment for Economic Empowerment by priming the economic pump; that is, directing some of the dollars they control to black-owned businesses in order to help them grow and expand the black business class.

Historically Black Colleges and Universities (HBCUs) must also play important roles as Primers. Leadership at HBCUs should, as much as possible, make it a practice to secure their products and services from black-owned businesses, especially those whose owners or managers graduated from their schools.

HBCUs are having difficult times keeping their doors open. Financial support from governmental sources is dissipating, while their graduates lag behind others in their contributions. Should we be supporting these institutions? Absolutely! But the leadership of HBCUs should study the procurement practices of their counterparts at white universities. Those institutions are very conscious of the laws of reciprocation.

Primer institutions are economic engines, and they must make a conscious effort to engage black businesses in their procurement processes. When you create wealthier alumni, you create a greater pool of potential contributors for development funds, scholarships, and academic programs.

HBCUs with business schools should also study black economics and wealth-building in the African-American community as part of their research. African-American businesses must build relationships with HBCUs to take advantage of the government-supported investments in fundamental science and research at these institutions. These research projects offer a potentially new knowledge base that black businesses and entrepreneurs can exploit to strengthen existing companies or to create new ones. We must convert this new knowledge into new jobs and new businesses so that the wealth will flow to our communities.

Lastly, the Primers with the potential for immediate and broad success in the African-American community are our religious houses of worship. These are the strongest institutions under the control of African-Americans, and contain the greatest concentration of blacks in our community. They are great sources of wealth. Churches and houses of worship, by their sheer collective numbers, can promote Economic Empowerment as well as influence African-Americans to reinvest dollars in their own community.

The black church is an Economic Harvest. It has the power to ease the famine in our communities. Just as the church played a major role in the Civil Rights Movement, it must hear this new call and release the harvest that can create a movement to transform the economic reality of our communities.

While many institutions in our communities have been destroyed or weakened over the years, the church remains a prevailing force. But black churches must continue to examine the economic realities of their existence, those of their congregations, and of the community they serve. Black churches have tremendous possibilities to effect change by utilizing the extensive financial resources that pass through their hands. They also have the power to simply encourage members to network and do business with each other and with black businesses in their communities.

According to the Bureau of Labor Statistics' Consumer Expenditure (CEX) for 2013, based on a survey of 15,732 households, the average annual black household contribution to religious organizations was $1,289. The 2010 census shows that there were 14.1 million black households in the United States. Combining these two statistics, we can conclude that black households annually contribute approximately $18.1 billion to religious organizations.

More specifically, fifty-nine percent of blacks belong to historically black churches, according to the Pew Research Center's 2009 report. Applying this statistic, we can conclude that black households annually contribute approximately $10.7 billion specifically to historically black churches. The black church must release this Economic Harvest in a way that will empower the communities that they serve.

PARTNERS: Corporate America and our black financial institutions

The term "partners" normally implies willing participants, but this component of the Circle of Wealth may be reluctant participants: Corporate America.

Members of Corporate America are keys to the Circle of Wealth because they have money—and a great deal of that money comes from African-Americans doing business with them.

For years, mostly white-owned companies have capitalized on the growing African-American consumer market. But these same companies feel little or no responsibility to channel any of the billions of dollars we spend annually with them back into growing or rebuilding our communities.

For example, banks hold billions of dollars in checking and savings accounts, certificates of deposit, credit cards, home mortgages, and auto loans belonging to African-Americans. But when it is time for blacks to access capital from those banks to start or expand businesses, we are turned down at rates that are disproportionate to whites and other racial and ethnic groups.

Leveraging our dollars

In many cities, these banks are no longer placing branches in our communities—leaving us to deal with loan sharks calling themselves "pawnshops" and "check-cashing establishments." This attitude on the banks' part displays a blatant disregard and disrespect for our dollars. They need to understand, in no uncertain terms, that a good partnership only works when it benefits both parties. This is an example of where the roles of the Messengers and Agitators can come into play.

Today our partnerships with financial institutions are not good ones—and that must change if we are to gain control of the economy in our community.

We must stop doing business with those who do not do business with us. And this includes banks and corporations who benefit from the billions of dollars we choose to spend with them each year. We must start leveraging our dollars so that when we do spend them, some of our money flows back to our community.

We must also insist that these banks and corporations actively use African-American businesses as vendors in their procurement processes. If they truly want to partner with us to help transform the economic reality of black America, then they must seriously ask themselves: "Are we removing the barriers, solving the problems, creating the solutions, and providing the opportunities that will enable black businesses to become full participants in our society and in our economy?" and "Is it in our long-term economic best interest to do so?" (The short answer to that is definitely "Yes!")

Our black financial institutions are also Partners in this equation.

Black financial institutions are nowhere near as strong as the major institutions—but if we are successful in converting political power to economic power, they stand to gain greatly.

Therefore, they too should be prepared to engage in this Economic Empowerment movement at every level, and not sit back and watch.

Converting political power to economic power is not a spectator sport; it is for those who want to get in the game, compete, and win.

Our black financial institutions should aggressively pursue the growth of African-American businesses, and then provide the level of service that will help retain them as customers. This group of Partners must come to understand that over time, they will get back what they give, and more. It makes good business sense to invest in developing a black business class, because it creates new markets and allows opportunities for reinvestment into areas that no one else is willing to invest in.

LEADERS: Strategists with strength and character to inspire others

Like their predecessors in the abolitionist and Civil Rights Movements, emerging Leaders in the Circle of Wealth are the ones who must orchestrate and lead this Historical Challenge.

Over the last fifty years, while we have made gains, for the most part we have witnessed a catastrophic failure of leadership like never before in the history of our people in America.

History has recorded it. Never before have we had so much power and yet done so little with it. Our leadership has been either unwilling or unable to meet our Historical Challenge.

Today we have black elected officials who have been serving in statehouses, in the U.S. Congress, and in other elected positions for twenty-five and thirty years. Yet the conditions of the people they represent have not changed; in fact, in many cases, the people are worse off today than they were when these individuals took office. Apparently, no one told these officials that they were elected because the people believed they could and would change their economic reality.

If you are a leader, but are not willing to take on the challenge of helping to grow black businesses so that they can help solve our people's problems, then you are simply an opportunist looking for opportunity, and lacking effective leadership qualities.

Today we require leadership with the capacity to awaken the people and unite us in a movement that will focus our attention, energy, and money on this twenty-first-century Historical Challenge.

So, the question for this new generation of black leaders is: are you willing to face our Historical Challenge—as those who have gone on before us did, when they faced their Historical Challenge—or will you leave it for another generation?

Leaders must:

- Be problem-solvers

- Include a new breed of well-informed and skilled decision-makers, and leaders in business, politics, and the community

- Be committed to setting a clear vision for converting political power to economic power

- Act consistently

- Focus on priorities that can improve the community

- Look toward the future

- Be unselfish in their dedication and commitment

This new leadership will have the responsibility of developing a black economic strategy that generates the kind of Economic Empowerment we need to transform lives and solve problems in our communities.

I believe that the vast majority of these new leaders are in the 25-45 age group. This new generation of leaders must be willing and able to take people where they may not want to go, but need to go.

These new leaders should be of such character, determination, and dedication that they will not rest until they are sure that the next generation has the opportunities and skills they need to achieve their own potential in the new global economy.

DRIVERS: The black business class

Drivers are the instrument for converting political power to economic power. Drivers are the engine of the new economy we must build: the black business class.

An economy exists when both buyers and sellers engage in perpetual exchange at a designated location. To control an economy, you must control the location and the exchange.

Businesses are the keys to changing the economic reality of a community because they are the points of exchange for money. The greater the opportunities (locations) for money to be exchanged, the longer the money remains in a community. When this process takes place in our communities, our property values increase, and our communities attract new residents and become magnets for diverse businesses and better paying jobs. The longer money stays in a community, the greater its impact on solving problems and building wealth. Unfortunately, in African-American communities, we control very few of the locations (businesses) where the exchanges (buying and selling) take place.

Building a viable black business class halts the vicious cycle of hopelessness.

A thriving black business class is the engine that drives an economy, and is therefore the key to economic stability. Any promised economic development that does not have the growth of the black business class as an objective is just an empty promise.

While the other six components of the Circle of Wealth are integral parts of the process, Drivers represent the critical piece that will help African-Americans achieve the kind of economic power that will spur growth and development in our communities.

Drivers propel the Economic Empowerment process because businesses, in general, tend to be self-sustaining and re-creating. Drivers give life to a community by acquiring wealth not only for their owners, but for other entities in the community as well.

A new generation of African-American companies

I'm not speaking of just any type of business, but a new generation of African-American companies, run by owners and managers armed with an unrelenting entrepreneurial spirit.

These businesses should be located in our communities and be able to take advantage of the latest innovations in information and technology. They should have the capacity to create high-quality jobs by producing valuable goods and services that can be sold inside our communities as well as around the world.

Issues, answers, and strategies

Are there issues to overcome in the creation of this new wave of businesses? The answer is an emphatic yes. Capital has always been an issue, and it will continue to be an issue for the foreseeable future. But we must leverage the political power, our savings, retirement, and family assistance when we cannot access the traditional sources.

I'm not suggesting that we simply assume that the traditional institutions will not finance our ideas, and that therefore we should not pursue those institutions. But if they are not willing to finance businesses in our communities, then we must cease doing business with them and call on others in our community to do the same.

African-Americans should no longer engage in commercial exchanges with those who only want a one-way transaction, with our money flowing their way. We must leverage our buying power to get the things we need to gain control of and grow the economy in our community.

In order for the Circle of Wealth to work, the monies must circulate from African-American entity to entity within our community. Creating an economy in our community requires us to be producers as well as consumers. We cannot offer this as an option in any commercial exchange; it must be a requirement for the relationship to exist in this new Economic Empowerment era.

A collective effort is critical to success.

I cannot overstate the importance of a collective effort by all sectors of the Circle of Wealth if we are going to convert political power to economic power in the African-American community.

In the Circle of Wealth, each of the components forms a direct link between a community vision and economic activity. In this case, the vision is that of Economic Empowerment. We are competing in a world where significant economic shifts are occurring. If we are going to succeed in this new world order, our politicians, our houses of worship, our business leaders, our local and national leaders, and our academic institutions must work together.

As Paul Robeson, Jr., wrote in *A Black Way of Seeing: From "Liberty" to Freedom*:

> The collective well-being is considered more important than the advancement of the individual. [. . .] Black Americans are a cohesive ethnic group with a distinct culture defined by historical experience. Our common bonds have been forged in the successive trials of slavery, enforced segregation, institutional racism, and the continued denial of equal opportunity.

Black executives-turned-entrepreneurs

Another issue, and one that I believe to be even more critical than access to capital, is the involvement of capable, skilled business owners and managers. These business leaders are essential for developing and growing a serious black business class.

I am convinced that the core leaders of this class are business executives who currently reside in or are now departing Corporate America.

Undoubtedly some leaders will be individuals fresh out of college, with either an undergraduate or a graduate business degree and a thirst for entrepreneurship. With few exceptions, however, they will lack the decision-making skills, credit-worthy experience, and crucial business relationships to provide the kind of business talent the Economic Empowerment movement needs at this juncture. However, these individuals should be tutored under the skilled wings of seasoned veterans, so when their time does come, they will be ready.

The new black business leadership we need now must come from those who have spent the last ten to twenty-five years in Corporate America, and have been seasoned as a result of building and managing some of America's greatest firms. They are experienced where it counts the most, in making decisions and solving problems. This is very important because, when reduced to its common denominator, business is about solving problems. When you solve people's problems, they pay you.

These black business leaders have cultivated their management skills, built relationships, and saved or invested enough money to have the initial capital necessary to start and grow their own businesses. They also have the ability to design and execute credible business strategies.

There are those of us who already understand the role that the black business class must play in converting political power to economic power. We must put that understanding to work today. We must seek out these black business leaders. We must encourage those with dreams of owning their own business to use the skills that they have developed in Corporate America. Once these black executives-turned-entrepreneurs start businesses, we must use our collective buying power to grow them. They are the key to our Economic Empowerment movement.

Controlling the critical forces

Just look at any American city with a high concentration of African-Americans. With few exceptions, each of them has the following in common:

- City leadership is black
- Boards and commissions are controlled by blacks, who control the budgets
- Little or no investment dollars are flowing into the inner cities, which have declined due to decay, crime, and high unemployment

• The majority of their business owners are not African-Americans

Why are these issues of concern? And what can we do about it?

Let's take the issue of no African-American business owners. If you are going to build economic power in your community, you must control the critical forces in the economic development process. Businesses are the points of exchange and the engines that keep the Circle of Wealth revolving. The way to keep the dollars in the black community is for blacks to control the places where the exchange takes place.

Let's take a one-dollar bill for an example.

• The dollar starts out in the hands of a black consumer; he or she spends it at the local supermarket.

• The supermarket keeps twenty cents of the dollar, and spends the eighty cents with the company that supplies its merchandise.

• This company keeps twenty cents, and spends the remaining sixty cents with the mechanic shop.

• The mechanic shop keeps forty cents, and spends the remaining twenty cents with his or her insurance agent.

This is an oversimplified version of how we spend our money, and with whom we spend it, but it demonstrates how a dollar flows through a community.

So what is the problem in the black community? In most cases, blacks own none of these businesses in their community. We cannot control this money-cycling process if we do not create or own the engine that drives it all: businesses.

The black public official in urban America

The other issue in these cities is even more disturbing. It is the case of Primer institutions controlled by black men and women who control billions of public dollars and make decisions on how they are spent.

Many of these tax dollars are collected from the very neighborhoods of their constituents who placed them in positions of authority and responsibility. I said earlier that most of these elected and appointed officials occupy their positions because of the civil rights struggle. Yet, these decision-makers tend to get amnesia when it comes to redistributing these tax dollars in ways that benefit their constituency.

How could they have such short memories and be so self-serving, when they can hear the cry of the people and can observe their deplorable conditions?

Are they blind to the harsh realities of the communities that they represent?

Do these black public officials not understand that reinvesting taxpayer dollars back into businesses in their communities helps to reverse decay and neglect, encourage investments, increase employment, halt decay, and reduce crime?

In fact, ensuring that black businesses are involved in the procurement process is one sure way that they can get public dollars back into the community they represent.

African-Americans who understand the Circle of Wealth concept must help these black public officials understand that solving problems in the poorest areas of their cities will take investment dollars, and that the officials themselves are the very people who have the power to make it happen by increasing spending with black businesses.

Jackson Mayor Harvey Johnson: The power of a disparity study for positive change

As Harvey Johnson, Jr., former two-term President of the National Conference of Black Mayors and three-term mayor of Jackson, Mississippi, once said, "The political leadership is going to have to focus on job creation as well as wealth creation" in the black community.

Johnson knows, because when he was elected mayor in 1997, he became the first African-American to lead Mississippi's capital city, where seventy percent of its almost 200,000 population is African-American.

Understanding the need to develop a stronger black business class, Mayor Johnson set out to increase the number of city contracts to African-Americans. His very first attempt landed the city in court, when a white contractor sued the city of Jackson and won.

The courts asserted that while there may be a disparity in the city's spending, the disparity must be demonstrated through a study of the city's procurement.

Undaunted, Johnson persevered.

The court loss led him to commission a disparity study. If the study could prove that racial discrimination had kept blacks at a historic economic disadvantage, the city could legally spend more of its dollars with black-owned businesses.

The study proved what everyone in Jackson, Mississippi, knew: a huge disparity existed in how the city spent its dollars. So Mayor Johnson developed and adopted court-approved policies to increase minority participation. Immediately, the city began to see the growth and development of a black business class. Black procurements in the city construction projects went from less than three percent to twenty-seven percent during Johnson's first administration.

While this increase may appear to be small, its potential impact is clear when viewed from a broader market context. I should know, because my information technology firm experienced tremendous growth as a result of Mayor Johnson's action.

And today, almost twenty years later, we are still experiencing growth.

Now it would be somewhat naive of me to expect cities and public bodies with major white leadership to conduct disparity studies and implement Equal Business Opportunity programs.

But when cities and other public bodies are overwhelmingly black in both population and leadership, I cannot comprehend their refusal to do disparity studies, or their choice to do a disparity study but not implement it.

Black decision-makers, counterproductive decisions

Let's take a look at the city and school district budgets for these five cities:

1. Detroit, Michigan
2. Jackson, Mississippi
3. Birmingham, Alabama
4. Atlanta, Georgia
5. Philadelphia, Pennsylvania

Four of the five cities have high majority black populations:
  Detroit, Jackson, Birmingham, and Atlanta

Four are led by African-American mayors:
  Jackson, Birmingham, Atlanta, and Philadelphia

Four have African-American majorities:

Detroit, Jackson, Birmingham, and Atlanta

Estimated total of city and school district budgets of these five cities combined:

$11.1 billion

Now imagine if these five cities spent just twenty-five percent of their combined city and school budgets to purchase products and services from black-owned businesses in their respective cities. Twenty-five percent of $11.1 billion is $2.775 billion a year!

Even at just ten percent annually, we are talking about adding $1.1 billion to the yearly bottom lines of black-owned businesses in these five cities.

This is the kind of power that African-Americans control, but the black decision-makers repeatedly make decisions that are counterproductive to the good of the communities and the people they serve. So crime continues to escalate, poverty flourishes, and decay digs in.

What are the answers?

Can these public and government entities provide all of the opportunities African-American businesses need? Absolutely not! However, these public bodies are the Primers in the Circle of

Wealth, and they must find a way to encourage the Drivers—the black business class—and support them in every way possible.

Without a black business class, there can be no Economic Empowerment for our communities. Without a black business class, we will fail to meet our Historical Challenge. Continuing in this way speaks doom for our communities and our economic future.

The call for twenty-first-century black leadership

African-Americans must demonstrate leadership in many ways during our twenty-first-century Historical Challenge to convert political power to economic power.

We must stand together and focus our collective efforts with wisdom and perseverance until we achieve economic power.

We need Messengers—journalists, writers, bloggers, pastors, professional athletes, actors and actresses, artists, singers and songwriters, politicians, and others with a platform— to spread the message of Silver Rights and Economic Empowerment.

We need Agitators—African-American fraternities, sororities, and social, business, and political organizations—to lobby and fight for our economic power.

We need Supporters—African-American consumers—to spend their dollars at black businesses in their communities.

We need Primers—Historically Black Colleges and Universities, our religious houses of worship, mayors' offices, city councils, and procurement offices—to direct their dollars to black businesses, support their constituents and alumni, and encourage members to do the same.

We need Partners—white and black financial institutions and corporations—to provide the level of service and capital required for black businesses and the black community to achieve economic power.

We need Leaders—African-American men and women with vision, strategy, the strength and wisdom to act, and the power to inspire others.

We need Drivers—men and women with unrelenting entrepreneurial spirits—to build businesses, create high-quality jobs, and produce valuable goods and services that can be sold inside our communities as well as around the world.

The Urgency of Now

The Civil Rights Movement has given us the freedom to take full advantage of the economic opportunities that other groups in this country have long enjoyed. Now, we must take advantage of those opportunities as part of our Historical Challenge and generational responsibility. Our immediate challenges are:

- Our individual willingness to change our spending habits
- The ability of the new black leadership to execute a strategy for economic power

In *Part III: Overcoming Our Historical Challenge*, you will see strategies that are already in action and producing results—strategies that *you* can use to convert political power to economic power in your community and beyond.

PART III:

Overcoming Our Historical Challenge

The Foundation for Solutions: Building the Black Business Class

Now is the time!

I say that the time has come for African-Americans to empower ourselves with the kind of collective wealth that will afford us the reinvestment dollars needed to solve the overwhelming problems in our communities.

We have very few problems that money will not solve. Communities grow when private dollars flow into them. The government's role is to create an environment conducive to economic growth—a role that it often plays out in other communities. Those leaders who represent us in government must become instruments for creating legislation that will empower people to solve problems. Those leaders must refrain from enacting policies that restrict people from meeting the challenges in their communities. We cannot and should not look to government to grow the economy in our communities. It is our responsibility; we must develop and control the economies in our communities, as others do in theirs. We must become the center point for problem-solving in our communities.

We have the power.

I want to make the distinction between our three Historical Challenges: our previous two challenges and the one that we're now engaged in.

The fundamental difference is that now we have the power to change. In the past, we had to use whatever resources we could find to convince the powers-that-be that we should not be slaves, that we have a right to vote, and that we have a right to public accommodations. Today we are in control of all of those things, control that resulted from the previous Historical Challenges being overcome.

So what do we do to meet this twenty-first-century Historical Challenge? We grow the black business class. Building the black business class is the component that will allow us to make the transition from political power to economic power.

A historical overview

The history of the black business class in twentieth-century America shows that we owe black businesses a lot. Black businesses existed long before African-Americans had any real political power. In fact, it was the black business class that helped finance the Civil Rights Movement—a movement that would later become a contributing factor to its decline.

In the Jim Crow era, the black business class was a necessity because African-Americans were not allowed in white establishments. Black businesses provided for our needs for food, shelter, clothing, housing, health care, transportation, education, social welfare, arts and entertainment, and personal and professional services. They were the centers for black employment and wealth, and made up the vast majority of the black middle class. Black businesses succeeded and flourished despite African-Americans' lack of political power.

All across this country, wherever there was a large black population, there were black business districts, which were the centers of commerce, entertainment, and religion for black people. During the day, they were thriving commercial districts; when the sun went down, they were transformed into centers of nightlife that rivaled any mainstream entertainment districts.

There was Harlem in New York; Birmingham, Alabama's Fourth Avenue business district; Farish Street in Jackson, Mississippi; the Jackson Ward neighborhood in Richmond, Virginia; 47th Street in Chicago, Illinois; and many more. At a time when we could not go to white businesses, everything that we needed had to come through black businesses.

Many of these black business districts included a series of nightclubs and theaters that were a part of the famous Chitlin' Circuit. Black performers such as Duke Ellington, Ella Fitzgerald, Bill "Bojangles" Robinson, Lena Horne, Cab Calloway, Billie

Holiday, Nat King Cole, James Brown, Sam Cooke, and others would perform, and black audiences would attend, because they were prohibited from attending white nightclubs. When entertainers traveled to various cities to perform, they were only allowed to stay in black hotels.

Through the Civil Rights Act of 1964 and the Voting Rights Act of 1965, blacks gained political power—and ironically, those gains rendered the black business class almost obsolete. The victories of the Civil Rights Movement enabled black consumers to venture outside of their own neighborhoods and shop at newly integrated businesses. This shift in spending by black consumers weakened the black business class, and also destroyed the economy that existed in black communities. When those businesses died from a lack of support, the black economy died.

It is an irrefutable fact that the successes of the Civil Rights Movement contributed to the demise of the black business class. I believe it was an unavoidable casualty in the twentieth-century challenge—a casualty dictated by the conditions of the time. But now we must use our political power to reverse this destructive outcome.

Today it is urgent that we grow the black business class of the twenty-first century.

The key component for the transition from political power to economic power is the black business class. That's why Where-

ToGo411.com was built: to grow the black business class. WhereToGo411.com is a national interactive business marketplace that connects black businesses to buyers, and it is integral to a twenty-first-century view of economic development.

I have owned an IT company for more than twenty-three years, and the single most important thing that I have had to focus on is growing my business. Regardless of the type or size of your business, there is only one way to grow your business: grow the revenue. So if I can connect you to revenue (buyers), then I'm dealing with your fundamental problem as a business owner. You'll still have to deal with how you manage that revenue, and everything else. But it doesn't help you to know how to *manage* the revenue if you're not *getting* the revenue. WhereToGo411.com connects African-American businesses to three types of buyers—black consumers, public, and corporate—using a technologically innovative online platform.

Economic Empowerment doesn't come from jobs.

In contrast to the twenty-first-century view of economic development, the traditional view currently subscribed to by the black leadership just doesn't work for solving the problems that exist in our community.

When most politicians, particularly black politicians, talk about economic development, they primarily talk about corporations coming in and bringing new jobs. However, Corporate

America is no longer setting up in our communities, which are perceived as high-risk areas. They set up in adjoining counties, where they perceive the risk for their investment as being much less.

And even if corporations do open facilities in our communities, the jobs they create will never generate the kind of Economic Empowerment that the people and the community need to transform the economic reality of the community. Those jobs will not create the kind of money that can be reinvested into the community, because the jobs are barely going to allow individuals to take care of their households.

Economic Empowerment doesn't come from jobs. Economic Empowerment is a function of ownership, principally businesses ownership. Only business ownership allows for money to circulate in a community. Business ownership builds excess capital for investment, creates employment opportunities, and ultimately leads to the acquisition of wealth.

Revenue and ripple effects

It's only because I own a business and produce excess income that I can employ people, give money to charitable causes, and take the lead in turning dollars around in the community. But if the black politicians and black leaders don't take actions to build the black business class, all those efforts will be in vain.

Here's an example of what I mean. A while back, I had a contract with the City of Jackson, Mississippi, a contract for about $200,000 per year. I had three employees working on that contract. I tithe to my church, and give to all kinds of community organizations and the university I attended, so that $200,000 contract was building the black business class, providing jobs, and circulating dollars in the community. Then a new African-American mayor came into office in Jackson. He took the contract away from me and gave it to a white firm in the adjoining county.

Here's the real issue about him taking the contract away from me and out of the community. My three employees were tied to that contract. I was able to give more to my church and community organizations because of that contract. So, while he viewed it as taking the contract away from me and my company, the fact is, he didn't just take it away from me—he took $200,000 a year out of the black community, and placed it in a community that he didn't even represent. His action caused me to lay off three people whose livelihoods were attached to that contract, and to eliminate the charitable contributions I made to the organizations I supported, too.

Those were the most obvious impacts from a business perspective, but there were also the ripple effects: the negative impacts for the families of my laid-off employees and for the organizations that counted on my support; and the reduction in the dollars circulating in our community, which negatively affected the people on a collective level.

We must become conscious consumers.

African-Americans have an annual buying power of $1.1 trillion—so we don't have a money problem per se. Our problem is how we spend our money, and with whom.

As consumers, we have massive buying power. As churches and leaders of organizations, we have great spending power. And as political leaders, we control policy that spends billions of dollars annually.

The only difference between a thriving community and a dying community is that in a thriving community, money is flowing into the community, and in a dying community, money is flowing out of the community. Economic Empowerment happens when you maintain or spend money in your community.

Oftentimes we spend our money with entities that invest the profits in elected officials and causes that directly oppose our achieving economic power. Instead, we must become conscious consumers seeking to spend our money in our community, and then follow our money through the buying process. We must understand what our dollar does after we spend it, and the impact that it has.

Don't fall prey to those who will call you racist because you are trying to change the economic reality of your community by spending money in a manner where it benefits you and your community. On one hand, they tell you that you should get off public assistance and pull yourself up by your bootstraps—but on the other hand, when you tell people to take responsibility and start spending their money with businesses in their community in order to solve problems in their community, they call you racist. They can't have it both ways.

Transforming the economic reality of our community starts with us. And there is only one way to accomplish this: we must grow the black business class.

The lifeblood of an economy

The economy is what really keeps a community alive. The lifeblood of an economy is the ability to have money circulate. If you don't have any businesses in your community, you can't have an economy there, because there's no place for the money to be exchanged. When black folks get a paycheck, they may bring it home for a minute, but they have to go back outside of their community to spend that money. That's why building the black business class is so critical.

Here's an example of how you build economic power through businesses. Assume that there are four of us, and each of us has a business. A customer comes in and spends $1.00 at Business A. Business A delivers the product or service to the customer. Now, it cost Business A $0.20 to deliver the product to that customer, and $0.80 to actually buy the product from Business B. So Business A has to pass $0.80 cents along to Business B.

Out of that $0.20 he's able to keep, Business A probably will be able to keep $0.05 to $0.10 as profit, then use that other $0.10 to cover the cost of operating his or her business. Business B gets the $0.80 from Business A. Business B takes $0.20 of the $0.80, and keeps $0.05 or $0.10 of it as profit. Business B takes the remaining $0.60 cents and spends it with Business C.

Business C takes $0.20 cents of the $0.60 cents, and keeps $0.05 to $0.10 cents as profit. Business C takes the remaining $0.40 cents and spends it with Business D. Business D takes $0.20 of the $0.40, and keeps $0.05 to $0.10 as profit. Business D takes that remaining $0.20 cents and, because there are no businesses in the community that sell goods or services that Business D needs, he or she has to go outside of the community and spend it elsewhere.

So out of the $1.00 the customer originally spent at Business A, $0.80 stays in that community and only $0.20 was spent outside of the community.

This is a simple definition of a functioning economy in a community. The longer your dollar remains in your community, the greater the opportunity for it to work to solve problems in said community.

But here's how it actually happens now. Without black businesses in the community, when you come in and spend that dollar with Business A, there is no Business B, Business C, or Business D. The dollar comes in at Business A, and it goes right back out. There is no way to gain profit and acquire wealth because there is no Business B, Business C, or Business D for the dollar to circulate through.

Building the black business class through the quote system

Black leaders and black politicians control tremendous political power because they control trillions of public dollars. There are laws that govern how they can spend those public dollars. In Mississippi, as in most states, there are basically three methods by which you could spend public dollars:

1. Request for bids

2. Request for qualifications (professional services)

3. Request for quotes

First is the request for bids. With this method, you essentially advertise the opportunity in major local publications, typically for large projects. The guidelines and requirements are usually very strict and the dollar amount tends to restrict bidding to the larger companies. In general, the issuing public body determines the specifications for the job; they post the opportunity online, or wherever is required by law in their state; they review the bids that come in; and they award the contract to one bidder. Usually, the lowest bid, or lowest and best, wins.

Second is the request for qualifications. This is usually a no-bid method. As a public official, with the request for qualifications, you're basically selecting who you want to provide a professional service. Professional services include legal services, architectural services, engineering services, and so on. You can reach out to people who are interested in providing that service, and they submit their qualifications to do the work. It's up to the decision-maker to select who they want—for the most part, it is subjective. Millions and millions of public dollars are spent this way.

Third is the request for quotes. A quote is a price that vendors charge for a product or service. Public agencies can seek quotes without a formal bid process when the cost is below an amount set by law. The request for quotes operates under a system that is similar state to state. In Mississippi, for instance, any public entity can request one quote and spend up to an amount not to exceed five thousand dollars. Any public entity can request two quotes and spend up to an amount not to exceed fifty thousand dollars by selecting one of those two quotes. Now fifty thousand dollars may not sound like a lot of money, but there are three things you need to consider.

First, public entities spend more money under the quote system than they do under bids and no-bids combined. And they spend that money every single day.

Secondly, the majority of African-American businesses can deliver at that fifty thousand dollar level and below. We don't have a lot of firms that can take on projects at the level of millions of dollars. But consider the fact that if a black business owner can get three or four quotes per month at fifty thousand dollars, that's two hundred thousand dollars per month, and $2.4 million per year. That creates cash flow for the business owner. And if business owners utilize cash flow to grow the business, their need to borrow money will be minimized.

Thirdly, in the quote system, the selection of a vendor is left up to the discretion of the buyer. As a buyer with public dollars to spend, I can buy from whomever I want to. I can just call anyone and spend up to an amount not to exceed five thousand dollars. I can call two business owners and I can spend up to an amount not to exceed fifty thousand dollars with one of them. This is the political power that we have as black elected and appointed officials when it comes to controlling and spending public dollars. Regrettably, very few of the calls for quotes are going to black businesses. But we can change this by using innovative technology like WhereToGo411.com's Quote, RFP, and Subcontracting Opportunities (QRSO) feature, which seamlessly allows buyers to send and receive quotes from African-American businesses.

Atlanta, 1974: Maynard Jackson establishes the model

The years 1964 and 1965 proved to be very pivotal years for African-Americans, laying the foundation for the emergence of major black leadership in America's cities.

Immediately following the passage of the Civil Rights Act of 1964 and the Voting Rights Act of 1965, black voter registration began to increase sharply. In 1965, 19.3% of blacks were registered to vote in Alabama, compared to 69.2% of whites. However, by 1988, more than 68% of blacks were registered to vote, compared to 75% of whites. It was even better in Louisiana, with 77% of blacks registered, compared to only 75% of whites.

These newly planted seeds would quickly produce great harvest when, in 1967, Carl Stokes was elected mayor of Cleveland, Ohio, thus becoming the first black mayor of a major U.S. city. Later that same year, Gary, Indiana, elected Richard Hatcher as its first black mayor. In the early 1970s, other major cities such as Detroit, Los Angeles, and Washington, D.C. also elected their first black mayors.

The first black mayor of a major southern city was Maynard Jackson, elected mayor of Atlanta, Georgia, in 1973. And it would be Maynard Jackson who would truly establish the model for using the gains of the Civil Rights Movement to convert political power to economic power and transform African-American businesses. In the process, he helped to grow a black business class in Atlanta that has never been equaled in another American city.

In 1974, Atlanta had started a $450 million project to expand Hartsfield Airport into an international airline hub. As the new mayor, Maynard Jackson informed the city's white business leaders that twenty-five percent of all contracts awarded in the project would be set aside for minority firms.

The new policy did not sit well with the white business leaders, who staunchly resisted it. For more than two years, they used every political and economic pressure at their disposal to snatch the project from Mayor Jackson's control. But Jackson would not budge from his position.

Using both diplomacy and strategy within the black and white communities, Mayor Jackson ultimately prevailed in 1976, when the white business leaders gave in and engaged in joint ventures with minority firms.

As a result of Atlanta's new policy, the proportion of total business the city did with minority-owned firms increased dramatically in five short years, from one percent in 1973 to more than thirty-nine percent by 1978. Today Atlanta is the nation's leader in black millionaires, with almost three times as many black general contractors as any other U.S. city.

Maynard Jackson embodied the new model of effective black leadership in the late twentieth century. However, Jackson's tenure as Mayor proved to be the exception, not the rule. Essentially, Jackson found himself in the right place at the right time to take advantage of economic opportunities created by the Civil Rights Movement—and he seized those opportunities. Sadly, many others who have since acquired political power have failed to convert their political power to economic power. They have not insisted on black businesses being a part of the procurement process in their cities.

The blueprint for today's black elected officials

The political power won by African-Americans in the 1970s, 1980s, and 1990s did translate into black economic power in Atlanta, but it did not translate similarly in other cities. Blacks as a whole were not able to take advantage of these opportunities. Efforts to convert black political power into economic power were not a calculated strategy, but happened in many cases in spite of the apathy of many political leaders. I believe the time has now come for cities where we control political power to make the growth of the black business class a primary focus. But this won't happen without effective leadership.

Maynard Jackson's use of the political process to grow and empower Atlanta's black business class is a blueprint for economic power in the African-American community—a blueprint that other cities with black political leadership must begin to follow.

U.S. Supreme Court decisions in the 1980s and 1990s prevent today's mayors from doing exactly what Maynard Jackson did in 1970s Atlanta. However, our twenty-first century leaders still have a responsibility to find ways to bring African-American businesses into the procurement process, as Maynard Jackson did in Atlanta, and as Harvey Johnson did in Jackson, Mississippi.

Using public funds to grow companies may be a recent phenomenon for African-American businesses, but it has been around as long as public dollars have been around. One would have to look long and hard to find a large white construction company that did not get its start from public contracting.

Today in the United States, there are over 500 black mayors, 43 black members in the U.S. House of Representatives, one black senator, and over 10,000 black elected officials. In many cities across the country, blacks also control boards, commissions, school districts, colleges and universities, and other entities where they have direct responsibility for procurement of goods and services.

In the twenty-first century, the key way to bring African-American businesses into the procurement process is to maximize the use of the quote system.

Since these dollars must be spent with somebody, why not spend some with African-American businesses, so that we can begin to build a solid business class armed with the capital to reinvest in our decaying communities?

We need our African-American leaders to step up and use the quote system to reinvest these dollars in the black community and solve the problems facing our inner cities.

We need our leaders to take charge and use the quote system to support inner-city businesses that reinvest in decayed buildings and employ people.

We need our political and business leaders to take responsibility and use the quote system to help create and support black-owned businesses, the places of exchange where black dollars can stop and circulate for a while in those communities.

After all, the reason that we elected these individuals is that we believed they would change our economic reality.

The blueprint for today's black business leaders

Just as the time has come for new Maynard-style political leaders in the twenty-first century, we now need a strong class of African-American business leaders, who are perhaps the most critical leadership component in this equation for converting political power to economic power.

I believe the conditions are ripe for this new group of leaders for several reasons. Firstly, more African-Americans are graduating from college than at any time in history. Secondly, we have more black professionals employed at the highest levels of Corporate America. Thirdly, the buying power of African-Americans is at an all-time high. And lastly, some of the greatest business minds in the African-American community are serving in America's greatest and wealthiest corporations.

Many of these great business leaders are approaching retirement. Some are being forced out through mergers, acquisitions, and downsizing. These African-Americans, who have polished their skills in Corporate America, must now take those skills and enter the ranks of business owners. In doing so, they will be ensuring the creation of a black business class like this country has never seen, and the building of a robust black economy like this country has never experienced.

Strategies in Action:
The Partnership for Economic Development

**Working together for a common purpose:
The Power of We!**

We have the power to solve the problems of failing schools, joblessness, and crime in our community, and we must begin to place ourselves at the center of change.

For years, we have waited and waited for others to come and solve our problems. By now it should be crystal clear: no one is coming. So we must do as we have always done in times of trouble—we must come together and solve our own problems. That is exactly what the Partnership for Economic Development (PED) is doing.

PED is a coalition dedicated to building the black business class and acquiring economic power for all African-Americans. PED is an alliance of like-minded people and organizations working together for this common purpose. We recognize the undeniable power that a committed group of people has to make historical changes in this country. As an alliance for combined action, PED Partners use various strategies to help stimulate economic development in the African-American community, through the growth of black businesses.

The Partnership has high regard for each participating organization as independent and having its own organizational mission. At the same time, we recognize that most organizations do include commitments to economic development within their mission statements.

At the core of any economic development strategy is the development of a business class.

Businesses are the sources of capital investment and the instruments that enable an economy to exist. Our community lacks capital investment, which is a primary byproduct of a strong business class. If we focus on growing black businesses, we will equip ourselves with the economic resources to solve the problems of our communities.

How does PED help to develop the black business class?

To fulfill our twenty-first-century Historical Challenge of converting political power to economic power, we must direct African-American consumers and leadership to African-American businesses.

The Partnership for Economic Development brings together many African-American entities such as fraternities, sororities, churches, faith-based institutions, black business groups, social organizations, government entities, nonprofits, and Historically Black Colleges and Universities. All of these entities support the achievement of our twenty-first-century Historical Challenge, and they have combined memberships numbering in the millions.

However, in the past, none of them had tools or instruments that could effectively direct their members to African-American businesses.

Today PED uses a tool that serves our common economic goals and helps build the black business class. This tool, which can be used by organizational leadership and consumers alike, is WhereToGo411.com.

WhereToGo411.com is a national, web-based, interactive business marketplace that directs consumers to African-American businesses, and connects buyers and vendors through its Quote, RFP, and Subcontracting Opportunities (QRSO) feature. Consumers can search the site for black businesses in their location. Government entities and private entities can use the site's unique QRSO feature to send and receive quotes, RFPs, and joint venture and subcontracting opportunities from black businesses. Corporations can use the application to expand their diversity spending. Large corporations seeking public contracts can use it when the public entity requires them to use minorities as sub-contractors.

How the PED coalition works

Each Partner benefits in many ways from participating in the PED coalition. For example, their organization becomes a key player in an economic development movement, and an instrument for greater problem-solving in the communities they serve. Their organization also has the potential for increase in revenue from the growth of their black businesses.

We want the effort to be very targeted and effective; therefore we encourage our organizational Partners to employ a specific strategy. For instance, we ask that they assess where they spend money, and measure their support of black businesses. We ask that they establish goals for spending money with black businesses, and urge them to lobby elected officials to increase spending with black businesses as an economic development strategy. We also ask that they use WhereToGo411.com as a tool to help achieve their organizational goals of economically empowering their members and the communities that they serve.

Spotlight on PED Partner, the Mississippi IHL Board of Trustees

The Mississippi Institutions of Higher Learning (IHL) Board of Trustees is a Partner in the PED coalition, expanding their minority spending via their Minority Economic Opportunity Initiative.

"The Board of Trustees has asked all of Mississippi's eight public universities to focus on diversity efforts," said Trustee Bob Owens, President of the Board of Trustees. "In addition to increasing diversity among students, faculty, and staff, we have also asked universities to seek ways to include more minority businesses in the bidding process when they request quotes and bids on goods and services."

The Board of Trustees has engaged WhereToGo411.com to help achieve this mission. Minority enterprises post information about their businesses and the goods and services they provide. Universities send and receive quotes, proposals, and subcontracting opportunities through the online system. This allows minority businesses to receive opportunities via the system (email), and be able to respond to the buyer by logging into the system and replying directly to the buyer with a price for the goods or services. This unique feature of WhereToGo411.com separates it from other tools directed at increasing opportunities for African-American businesses.

"The Minority Economic Opportunity Initiative is an important step forward in reaching the Board of Trustees' goal of increasing diversity on our university campuses," said Trustee C.D. Smith, Chair of the Board's Diversity Committee. "The website is a great tool to give both the universities and the minority businesses the information they need to access the opportunities to work together. Our goal is to expand opportunities and help minority businesses to grow and thrive."

While any business can be listed on the site, African-American businesses are recruited for inclusion in the Featured Listing section, which provides them access to the QRSO solicitations.

The procurement officers on each university campus received training on how to post opportunities to the site, and how to use the site to retrieve quotes and information from the vendors.

"The ability to use the site to request quotes and track the outcome, including when a vendor does or does not submit a proposal and whether the vendor receives the bid, will save our universities time and effort," said Dr. Hank M. Bounds, Commissioner of Higher Education. "It will also provide data for future decision-making."

Mississippi Public Universities utilize a number of tools to reach out to minority businesses, including holding minority vendor fairs on campus. WhereToGo411.com provides another tool, and allows for a connection and interaction to occur long after the vendor fair concludes.

In addition to IHL, PED has Partnerships with the City of Jackson, Mississippi, and with Hinds County. Both of those entities, controlled by African-Americans, are excellent examples of using WhereToGo411.com to convert political power to economic power.

Spotlight on the Gospel of Silver Rights (The Other Good News): Summits for Church and Business Leaders

PED convenes Gospel of Silver Rights Summits for clergy and business owners. A Gospel of Silver Rights Summit is a call to action to engage a strategy to grow black businesses by connecting them to the massive Economic Harvest of the church.

Some pastors have questioned the use of the term "Gospel," and they certainly have the right to do so. But my hope is that they would focus their energy and resources on the concept and the problem that we are trying to solve.

Because in spite of our political gains since the 1960s, today in virtually every urban community across America, urban decay is at its peak; there is a proliferation of crime; hundreds of thousands of black men are caught up in the criminal justice system; and joblessness has become an accepted norm.

Many people will have you believe that these are mere social issues that we should wait on government to solve. But we know that these are not social issues; they are economic issues with social consequences. And we know there are solutions. Fortunately, where there is faith, there is hope—and this is the other good news, the Gospel of Silver Rights.

Releasing the economic harvest of the church to help grow black businesses

> *It's all right to talk about long white robes over yonder, in all of its symbolism. But ultimately people want some suits and dresses and shoes to wear down here!*
>
> *It's all right to talk about streets flowing with milk and honey, but God has commanded us to be concerned about the slums down here, and his children who can't eat three square meals a day.*
>
> *It's all right to talk about the new Jerusalem, but one day, God's preacher must talk about the new New York, the new Atlanta, the new Philadelphia, the new Los Angeles, the new Memphis, Tennessee. This is what we have to do.*
>
> —Dr. Martin Luther King, Jr., April 3, 1968, Memphis, Tennessee

There can be no economic transformation without the growth of the black business class. That is the motivation for a Gospel of Silver Rights Summit.

Why the church?

Historically black churches have an annual spending power of $10.7 billion. Historically black churches consistently have access to the largest audience that gathers in black communities, with an estimated consumer buying power of over $1 trillion. The pastors have clout and influence. Their congregations consist of many of the business owners in the community. The black church must release this Economic Harvest. It has the power to ease the famine in our communities.

Why black businesses?

Just as the Civil Rights Movement was critical to African-Americans' acquiring political power, the black business class is the instrument for achieving economic power.

A strong black business class is the engine that drives an economy, and is therefore the key to economic stability. When the economy is thriving in our communities, property values increase, and our neighborhoods attract new residents and become magnets for diverse businesses and better-paying jobs.

Twenty-first-century technology is critical here. It is the catalyst that can instantaneously connect forward-thinking leaders during this time of economic turmoil in America. For instance, as the go-to national interactive business marketplace, WhereToGo411.com maximizes today's technology to promote Economic Empowerment in the black community.

"Economic Development through the Black Church" with the A.M.E. Church

Some church leaders have already partnered with business leaders and made joint commitments to economic development goals. For instance, in late 2014, the A.M.E. Church's Second District held a special Economic Empowerment session, "Economic Development through the Black Church," with the priority on identifying ways that black churches can help build the black business class. Church leaders and business leaders in the A.M.E.'s Second District (North Carolina, Virginia, Maryland, and D.C.) participated in the session.

From that meeting, A.M.E. pastors created a strategy for 2015. They hope it will quickly become a model that is used by other denominations and by African-American consumers across the country.

The A.M.E. strategy is for its Second District churches to support two black-owned businesses—a car dealership and a chain of restaurants—for the year 2015. Church members are interested in and amenable to the strategy.

As members patronize the two businesses, those sales will be tracked for the churches' benefit. The hopes are that these Economic Empowerment partnerships will be successful; that they will inspire other A.M.E. districts to launch similar strategies; and that this growing Economic Empowerment movement will inspire other denominations to launch strategies to help build the black business class.

Similarly, the family of Maggie Anderson of Chicago, Illinois, set out to purchase as much as they could from black businesses for an entire year. According to Anderson, they felt that they should be spending more money with black businesses, so she and her family did everything that they could to do so.

With individual strategies being adopted for growing black businesses, part of the problem is finding a tool that can connect those businesses to buyers. While Maggie Anderson and her family should be commended for their effort to further advance this notion, it is just not practical to expect black consumers, in great numbers, to do what they did.

That is why we created WhereToGo411.com. It has global reach and can be used by any group anywhere to connect to black businesses in their local area. The A.M.E. strategy, while it is also an excellent step in the right direction, is limited to the support of just two black businesses, because that is all that they can manage with the strategy. We would hope that the A.M.E.

church would consider a partnership with WhereToGo411.com, which can manage an unlimited number of buyers-to-business transactions and relationships.

Convening a Gospel of Silver Rights Summit in your community

PED convenes Gospel of Silver Rights Summits for church and business leaders to engage in dialogue about how to build a black business class that's capable of sustaining an economy in urban communities. The goal of each Summit is to formulate a strategy that involves black churches and other organizations in releasing their Economic Harvest, in an effort to help grow black businesses and transform the economic reality of the communities they serve. Keynote speakers focus on the value of the church releasing its Economic Harvest, and introduce methodology for a sustained strategy for the church's role in the growth of black businesses.

There can be no economic transformation of a community without a strong business class.

PED needs strong partners, buyers, consumers, and black businesses to drive economic development. Check out the following pages to find out how *you* can help convert political power to economic power with the PED coalition.

Be a PED Messenger

You can be a Messenger for the PED coalition if you are:

- A member of the black media
- A black journalist working in mainstream media
- A black political leader, national or local
- A religious leader
- An artist, songwriter, musician, poet, blogger, or other creator
- Someone with the power to influence our culture at the local and national levels

As a Messenger, you can use your expertise in communications to craft effective messages about the Partnership for Economic Development, the work we're doing, and the opportunities we offer to black businesses. You can transmit those messages to African-Americans via the media and in the venues where you work and interact with people on a daily basis.

As a Messenger, you can find ways to use your communications skills and the power of information to carry the message of economic power, and help shape it as the highest priority for African-Americans in the twenty-first century.

Be a PED Agitator

You can be an Agitator for the PED coalition if you are a leader or member of a black:

- Fraternity
- Sorority
- Faith-based organization
- Social organization
- Professional organization
- Political organization
- Business

The most important action an Agitator can take? Join forces with the Partnership for Economic Development to help stimulate economic development in the African-American community through the growth of black businesses. As part of the PED coalition, your organization will become a key player in an economic development movement, and an instrument for greater problem-solving in communities you serve.

As an Agitator, you can also support the PED coalition in these ways:

- Assess where your organization spends money
- Establish goals for spending money with black businesses

- Measure your organization's support of black businesses
- Identify black businesses within your organization
- Lobby elected officials to increase spending with black businesses as an economic development strategy
- Participate in a Gospel of Silver Rights Summit in your community
- Maximize your organization's use of WhereToGo411.com

Be a PED Supporter

As a consumer, you can be a Supporter of the PED coalition in these ways:

- Assess where you spend money
- Establish goals for spending money with black businesses
- Measure your support of black businesses
- Lobby elected officials to increase spending with black businesses as an economic development strategy
- Use WhereToGo411.com to search for black businesses in your location.

Be a PED Primer

You can be a Primer for the PED coalition if you work at a public or private entity that African-Americans directly control, including:

- Public school board
- College or university, especially a Historically Black College or University
- Supervisor's or commissioner's office
- Mayor's office
- City council
- Procurement office that buys products and services for these entities, institutions, and elected bodies

The most important action a Primer can take? Join forces with the Partnership for Economic Development to help stimulate economic development in the African-American community through the growth of black businesses. As part of the PED coalition, your organization will become a key player in an economic development movement and an instrument for greater problem-solving in communities you serve.

As a Primer, you can also support the PED coalition in these ways:

- Assess where your organization spends money
- Establish goals for spending money with black businesses
- Measure your organization's support of black businesses
- Lobby elected officials to increase spending with black businesses as an economic development strategy
- Participate in a Gospel of Silver Rights Summit in your community
- Maximize your organization's use of WhereToGo411.com

Be a PED Partner

You can be a Partner with the PED coalition if you are a:

- Leader in Corporate America, especially a white-owned company or white financial institution
- Leader at a black financial institution

The most important action a Partner can take? Join forces with the PED coalition to help stimulate economic development in the African-American community through the growth of black businesses. As part of the coalition, your organization will become a key player in an economic development movement and an instrument for greater problem-solving in communities you serve.

As a Partner, you can also support the PED coalition in these ways:

- Assess where your organization spends money
- Establish goals for spending money with black businesses
- Measure your organization's support of black businesses
- Lobby elected officials to increase spending with black businesses as an economic development strategy

- Participate in a Gospel of Silver Rights Summit in your community
- Maximize your organization's use of WhereToGo411.com

Be a PED Leader

You can be a Leader with the PED coalition if you are a:

- Strategist with strength and character to inspire others
- Leader who is committed to converting political power to economic power in the African-American community
- Well-informed decision-maker in business, politics, or the community
- Visionary leader who is willing and able to take people where they may not want to go, but need to go

The most important action a Leader can take? Join forces with the Partnership for Economic Development to help stimulate economic development in the African-American community through the growth of black businesses. As part of the PED coalition, your organization will become a key player in an economic development movement and an instrument for greater problem-solving in communities you serve.

As a Leader, you can also support the PED coalition in these ways:

- Assess where your organization spends money
- Establish goals for spending money with black businesses
- Measure your organization's support of black businesses

- Lobby elected officials to increase spending with black businesses as an economic development strategy

- Participate in a Gospel of Silver Rights Summit in your community

- Maximize your organization's use of WhereToGo411.com

Be a PED Driver

You can be a Driver with the PED coalition if you are a:

- Member of the black business class

- Part of the new generation of African-American companies run by owners and managers armed with an unrelenting entrepreneurial spirit

The most important action a Driver can take? Join forces with the PED coalition to help stimulate economic development in the African-American community through the growth of black businesses. As part of the PED coalition, your organization will become a key player in an economic development movement and an instrument for greater problem-solving in communities you serve.

As a Driver, you can also support the PED coalition in these ways:

- Assess where your organization spends money

- Establish goals for spending money with black businesses

- Measure your organization's support of black businesses

- Lobby elected officials to increase spending with black businesses as an economic development strategy

- Participate in a Gospel of Silver Rights Summit in your community

- Maximize your organization's use of WhereToGo411.com

Contact:

The Partnership for Economic Development

620 North State Street, Suite 304

Jackson, MS 39202

Email: partners@wheretogo411.com

Phone: 769.553.1978

Strategies in Action:
More About WhereToGo411.com

WhereToGo411.com is a national, web-based, interactive business marketplace that helps grow African-American businesses by connecting them to local and national buyers. The website was created to help facilitate a national strategy for economic development in urban communities through the growth of black businesses.

Business owners can list their businesses on WhereToGo411.com, along with a description, product images, video, and coupons where buyers are able to easily find them and secure their products and services. Consumers can search the site for black businesses in their location. Government entities and private entities can use the site's unique QRSO (Quote, RFP, and Subcontracting Opportunities) feature to send and receive quotes, RFPs, and subcontracting opportunities from black businesses.

Where ToGo411.com helps to create relationships between African-American businesses and major buyers such as local and national companies, government agencies, private entities, and public economic engines, including Historically Black Colleges and Universities, seats of governments, school boards, counties, and airport authorities. These public and private buyers spend billions of dollars annually and have engaged WhereToGo411.com to help identify and connect them to black businesses.

A primary mission of WhereToGo411.com is to help major buyers meet and even exceed their diversity spending goals. The site is equipped to track spending, including the number of quotes sent and approved, and responses when the vendor does not accept the quote.

Our dedication to this cause is driven by an ardent passion, as well as the belief that black businesses are the instruments for transforming the economic realities of African-American communities. For us, it's about something much bigger than just increasing sales and revenue. It's about solving problems.

The Future Starts Now

In each of the past two centuries, African-Americans have had to face Historical Challenges. And they were able to overcome these challenges through major movements guided by faithful, competent, and unrelenting leadership. However, in the twenty-first century, civil rights is no longer the dominant challenge facing African-Americans. That battle was won, finally, in the twentieth century. The new issue is Silver Rights (Economic Empowerment) and, as African-Americans did in the last two centuries, we must meet this Historical Challenge head-on. We must convert our political power to economic power.

The emergence and evolution of the Internet allows us to live in a time of great innovation, excitement, and unique opportunities to build economic power. It has changed the way we live, learn, work, play, and communicate with each other—by connecting anyone to anyone, and to anything and everything. For many, the Internet represents the greatest tool of all time for leveling the playing field for all who choose to embrace it. Its impact over time will be greater than the Industrial Revolution of the nineteenth century. The Internet is redefining how we shop and do business in the new global economy.

This digital revolution of the twenty-first century is at the core of a growing world economy, with more than two billion users, including hundreds of millions of users in the United States alone. The Gartner Group reports that online Business-to-Business (B2B) is a multi-trillion-dollar market. Internet research firm comScore says that online Business-to-Consumer (B2C) spending is in the hundreds of billions of dollars per year, and continues to grow.

It is this impact on commerce that caused me to engage the Internet as my instrument for increasing wealth through entrepreneurship and business ownership, using WhereToGo411.com as an online tool.

The Internet gives businesses that are willing to embrace it a competitive advantage. Ultimately, it will set the rules for deciding the winners and the losers in this new era. Many companies today are placing more value on their digital assets than they are on their physical assets, because the Internet allows you to lower your overhead for buying, selling, and marketing your goods. You would be hard-pressed to match the affordable cost of setting up an Internet-based business with the cost of establishing a traditional, expensive, brick-and-mortar business.

Make no mistake: the key to success in the Internet economy

will be an enterprise's ability to use Internet technology to satisfy customers, improve productivity, reduce time to market, increase revenue, and build relationships. If we are going to tap into the over $1 trillion African-American market, then we must build the infrastructure that allows these consumers (i.e., us) to obtain information, request support, complete business transactions, and place orders 24/7. Nothing does that like the Internet. WhereToGo411.com is helping to build such an infrastructure for African-American businesses.

Today information is king, and access to it empowers employees, customers, and business partners to work more effectively while making decisions based on current and relevant information.

As a national coalition of economic growth engines, the Partnership for Economic Development focuses on growing black businesses using a new economic strategy. While I offer it as a means for building the black business class, clearly it represents only one way of converting our political power to economic power.

The Circle of Wealth concept represents another way. If we are going to succeed in creating this historic movement in the twenty-first century, then we must engage all seven components of the Circle of Wealth.

The Gospel of Silver Rights provides another approach, one that brings African-American church leaders and business leaders together to reap the church's Economic Harvest.

For my part, I will continue to be an Agitator and a Driver in the Circle of Wealth, using WhereToGo411.com's success to influence political and corporate business leaders in positions of authority to make decisions that will increase procurement opportunities for African-American businesses.

We will encourage the African-American leaders of our time to follow the example of the late Maynard Jackson, who had authority and the courage to exercise it to ensure that African-American businesses were involved in that multimillion-dollar Atlanta airport expansion project. It is said that Maynard Jackson's actions led directly to the creation of more than twenty black millionaires, and indirectly to the creation of twenty more.

African-Americans must work together to explore other answers as well. What actions are you, your church, business, or organization taking? What initiatives are you trying to launch? Let us know! We may be able to come to your location to help develop a strategy and provide training that will help grow the black businesses class in your community.

Now I know there are some who believe that we do not need to gain economic power or build the black business class. I suspect that there are even those who consider this book and its central message to be racist. And yes, there will be some affluent

African-Americans who will view the Circle of Wealth concept as unnecessary—and I do understand why they think as they do. Many affluent blacks no longer live in or near the inner cities, with the cities' trials and tribulations, and have therefore become deaf to the cries of the hungry child who cannot sleep. They are not familiar with elderly ladies who must make the choice between paying their utility bills and purchasing their medications. Nor are they aware of the family of five who lives below the poverty line while both parents work full-time, or the working-poor family who still cannot afford health care for their sick child.

But this book is not about wallowing in black self-pity.

This book is about developing an economic movement that will build the kind of economic power that will allow us to reverse these depressing conditions in our inner-city communities.

This book is a call to action to those with the talent and skills, the sense of historic mission and responsibility, and the willingness to embrace this challenge with the spirit, passion, and commitment of those who paved the way for us.

So, in closing, I ask these questions: Why shouldn't African-Americans create a national strategy for converting political power to economic power, when the conditions of our people in the inner cities cry out for us to do so? If not us, then who?

It is our responsibility, our problem. We must solve it.

For those of you who would say, "It cannot be done," I say, "Let's try."

For those who say, "We have already tried," I say, "Let's try again."

There is no time to waste. We must use the "Power of We" to embrace the urgency of now. We must begin today.

Acknowledgments

It is at the height of admiration and with eternal appreciation that I acknowledge individuals who have selflessly contributed to this urgent and timely piece of work. While I will acknowledge three individuals, it does not come close to exhausting the list of individuals who have had an impact on the ideas and concepts included in the book.

Let me begin by thanking Nicole for her energy, enthusiasm, focus, dedication, commitment, and organizational skills that were there from the beginning of the project. Your ardent appreciation for effectual journalism and your life experiences helped to add great value and structure to this work. While I am a published author, at my core I'm simply a businessman, and am much better at solving problems than I am at articulating directions and visions for my people. So I thank you for helping to make this work worthy of deliberation by those who would dare to engage it. It is, in my view, a cosmic improvement over my first book, *From Civil Rights To Silver Rights: We Need An Economic Movement*, which was an attempt to move African-Americans from a dominant focus on Civil Rights to that of Silver

Rights, and to incite a new movement that would redirect our energies toward the acquisition of wealth as a dominant challenge. Lastly, I want to thank you for pushing me, in very subtle ways, to write even when I thought that I didn't have the time or energy to do so. I can't begin to tell you how many times I arrived home with seemingly nothing left, only to open an email to find an assignment from you wrapped in encouragement.

Kathy Times, a two-time Emmy Award-winning broadcast journalist, who at the apex of her career and after leading the largest journalist organization of color in America, chose to buy into this Historical Challenge, at great sacrifice of personal finance and health, rather than pursuing opportunities that would have delivered greater personal, professional, and financial gains. Your people and I owe you a great deal of veneration and gratitude. While I was crafting out ideas and concepts like WhereToGo411.com, you were using your relationships to convert it into a useful tool to help grow African-American businesses. Your efforts and contributions have allowed me to understand that ideas are simply unrealized materialism until they are manifested through practical actions.

Lastly, there is Dr. Adana Llanos, a young female African-American cancer research scientist and assistant professor of Epidemiology at a major level-one cancer research institute on the East Coast. Having authored and co-authored more than fifteen papers, Dr. Llanos is developing new approaches to the detection, treatment, and prevention of cancer through cutting-edge clinical, basic, population, and translational research. Her professional credentials, research, and published studies elevate her to heights seldom imagined, let alone achieved by individuals of her age, gender, or race. Although immersed in your very critical research to identify ways to save lives, you vowed to be a part of this work, and I'm very delighted that you did. Yes, you are a woman of your word, and I thank you for providing final editing for this work and recognizing its urgency.

Finally, I have but one more request: that you would continue to do all that you can while you can to push this generation towards achieving this Historical Challenge. God Bless!

About James Covington

For over twenty-five years, James Covington has had a singular focus on entrepreneurship. In addition to being the President of WhereToGo411.com, Covington is President of iVision IT Consultants, an information technology firm that offers innovative IT solutions to help companies leverage their brands and expand their market reach.

Covington's first book, *From Civil Rights to Silver Rights*, laid the groundwork for an Economic Empowerment movement for African-Americans. In this sequel, Covington issues an urgent call to action: a call to understand the Historical Challenge we face as African-Americans, to understand what we must do to overcome the challenge, and to overcome it—by growing a black business class that can empower us to convert our political power to economic power.

www.ingramcontent.com/pod-product-compliance
Lightning Source LLC
Chambersburg PA
CBHW070856180526
45168CB00005B/1845